Extreme Closeup

Paul Borthwick

Mark Syswerda

David C. Cook Publishing Co.
Elgin, Illinois—Paris, Ontario

Custom Curriculum
Extreme Closeup

© 1994 David C. Cook Publishing Co.

Published by David C. Cook Publishing Co.
850 North Grove Ave., Elgin, IL 60120
Cable address: DCCOOK
Series creator: John Duckworth
Series editor: Randy Southern
Editor: Randy Southern
Option writers: Stan Campbell, John Duckworth, Sue Reck, and Randy Southern
Designer: Bill Paetzold
Cover illustrator: Kevin Pope
Inside illustrator: Joe Weissmann
Printed in U.S.A.

ISBN: 0-7814-5165-5

CONTENTS

Sessions by Mark Syswerda
Options by Stan Campbell, John Duckworth, Sue Reck, and Randy Southern

About the Authors

Mark Syswerda is an associate editor of youth products at David C. Cook. In addition to working with youth groups, he has contributed to such youth resources as the *Quick Studies B.C.* and *Great Groups* series (David C. Cook).

Stan Campbell has been a youth worker for almost twenty years and has written several books on youth ministry including the BibleLog series (SonPower) and the Quick Studies series (David C. Cook). Among the books he's written in the Custom Curriculum series are *Hormone Helper, Just Look at You! What Would Jesus Do?* and *Your Bible's Alive!* Stan and his wife, Pam, are youth directors at Lisle Bible Church in Lisle, Illinois.

John Duckworth is a writer and illustrator in Carol Stream, Illinois. He has worked with teenagers in youth groups and Sunday school, written several books including *The School Zone* (SonPower) and *Face to Face with Jesus* (in the Custom Curriculum series), and created such youth resources as Hot Topics Youth Electives and Snap Sessions for David C. Cook.

Sue Reck is an editor for Chariot Family Products. She is also a free-lance curriculum writer. She has worked with young people in Sunday school classes, youth groups, and camp settings.

Randy Southern is a product developer of youth material at David C. Cook and the series editor of Custom Curriculum. He has also worked on such products as Quick Studies, Incredible Meeting Makers, Snap Sessions, First Aid for Youth Groups, Junior Highs Only, and Pathfinder Electives.

You've Made the Right Choice!

Thanks for choosing **Custom Curriculum!** We think your choice says at least three things about you:

(1) You know your group pretty well, and want your program to fit that group like a glove;

(2) You like having options instead of being boxed in by some far-off curriculum editor;

(3) You have a small mole on your left forearm, exactly two inches below the elbow.

OK, so we were wrong about the mole. But if you like having choices that help you tailor meetings to fit your kids, **Custom Curriculum** *is* the best place to be.

Going through Customs

In this (and every) **Custom Curriculum** volume, you'll find

• five great sessions you can use anytime, in any order.

• reproducible student handouts, at least one per session.

• a truckload of options for adapting the sessions to your group (more about that in a minute).

• a helpful get-you-ready article by a youth expert.

• clip art for making posters, fliers, and other kinds of publicity to get kids to your meetings.

Each **Custom Curriculum** session has three to six steps. No matter how many steps a session has, it's designed to achieve these goals:

• *Getting together.* Using an icebreaker activity, you'll help kids to be glad they came to the meeting.

• *Getting thirsty.* Why should kids care about your topic? Why should they care what the Bible has to say about it? You'll want to take a few minutes to earn their interest before you start pouring the "living water."

• *Getting the Word.* By exploring and discussing carefully selected passages, you'll find out what God has to say.

• *Getting the point.* Here's where you'll help kids make the leap from principles to nitty-gritty situations they are likely to face.

• *Getting personal.* What should each group member do as a result of this session? You'll help each person find a specific "next step" response that works for him or her.

Each session is written to last 45 to 60 minutes. But what if you have less time—or more? No problem! **Custom Curriculum** is all about . . . options!

What Are My Options?

Every **Custom Curriculum** session gives you fourteen kinds of options:

• *Extra Action*—for groups that learn better when they're physically moving (instead of just reading, writing, and discussing).

• *Combined Junior High/High School*—to use when you're mixing age levels, and an activity or case study would be too "young" or "old" for part of the group.

• *Small Group*—for adapting activities that would be tough with groups of fewer than eight kids.

• *Large Group*—to alter steps for groups of more than twenty kids.

• *Urban*—for fitting sessions to urban facilities and multiethnic (especially African-American) concerns.

• *Heard It All Before*—for fresh approaches that get past the defenses of kids who are jaded by years in church.

• *Little Bible Background*—to use when most of your kids are strangers to the Bible, or haven't made a Christian commitment.

• *Mostly Guys*—to focus on guys' interests and to substitute activities they might be more enthused about.

• *Mostly Girls*—to address girls' concerns and to substitute activities they might prefer.

• *Extra Fun*—for longer, more "rowdy" youth meetings where the emphasis is on fun.

• *Short Meeting Time*—tips for condensing the session to 30 minutes or so.

• *Fellowship & Worship*—for building deeper relationships or enabling kids to praise God together.

• *Media*—to spice up meetings with video, music, or other popular media.

• *Sixth Grade*—appearing only in junior high/middle school volumes, this option helps you change steps that sixth graders might find hard to understand or relate to.

• *Extra Challenge*—appearing only in high school volumes, this option lets you crank up the voltage for kids who are ready for more Scripture or more demanding personal application.

Each kind of option is offered at least twice in each session. So in this book, you get *almost 150* ways to tweak the meetings to fit your group!

Customizing a Session

All right, you may be thinking. *With all of these options flying around, how do I put a session together? I don't have a lot of time, you know.*

We know! That's why we've made **Custom Curriculum** as easy to follow as possible. Let's take a look at how you might prepare an actual meeting. You can do that in four easy steps:

(1) *Read the basic session plan.* Start by choosing one or more of the goals listed at the beginning of the session. You have three to pick from: a goal that emphasizes *knowledge,* one that stresses *understanding,* and one that emphasizes *action.* Choose one or more, depending on what *you* want to accomplish. Then read the basic plan to see what will work for you and what might not.

(2) *Choose your options.* You don't *have* to use any options at all; the

basic session plan would work well for many groups, and you may want to stick with it if you have absolutely no time to consider options. But if you want a more perfect fit, check out your choices.

As you read the basic session plan, you'll see small symbols in the margin. Each symbol stands for a different kind of option. When you see a symbol, it means that kind of option is offered for that step. Turn to the options section (which can be found immediately following the Repro Resources for each session), look for the category indicated by the symbol, and you'll see that option explained.

Let's say you have a small group, mostly guys who get bored if they don't keep moving. You'll want to keep an eye out for three kinds of options: Small Group, Mostly Guys, and Extra Action. As you read the basic session, you might spot symbols that tell you there are Small Group options for Step 1 and Step 3—maybe a different way to play a game so that you don't need big teams, and a way to cover several Bible passages when just a few kids are looking them up. Then you see symbols telling you that there are Mostly Guys options for Step 2 and Step 4—perhaps a substitute activity that doesn't require too much self-disclosure, and a case study guys will relate to. Finally you see symbols indicating Extra Action options for Step 2 and Step 3—maybe an active way to get kids' opinions instead of handing out a survey, and a way to act out some verses instead of just looking them up.

After reading the options, you might decide to use four of them. You base your choices on your personal tastes and the traits of your group that you think are most important right now. **Custom Curriculum** offers you more options than you'll need, so you can pick your current favorites and plug others into future meetings if you like.

(3) *Use the checklist.* Once you've picked your options, keep track of them with the simple checklist that appears at the end of each option section (just before the start of the next session plan). This little form gives you a place to write down the materials you'll need, too—since they depend on the options you've chosen.

(4) *Get your stuff together.* Gather your materials; photocopy any Repro Resources (reproducible student sheets) you've decided to use. And . . . you're ready!

The Custom Curriculum Challenge

Your kids are fortunate to have you as their leader. You see them not as a bunch of generic teenagers, but as real, live, unique kids. You care whether you really connect with them. That's why you're willing to take a few extra minutes to tailor your meetings to fit.

It's a challenge to work with real, live kids, isn't it? We think you deserve a standing ovation for taking that challenge. And we pray that **Custom Curriculum** helps you shape sessions that shape lives for Jesus Christ and His kingdom.

—The Editors

How You and God Can Stay Connected

by Paul Borthwick

Several years ago, my sister-in-law returned home after a meal out at a local restaurant. A few hours later, she was overcome with nausea. Her first thought? Food poisoning. She quickly grabbed the telephone directory, searching for the number for the "Poison Control Hotline."

By the time she found the number, she felt so sick that she thought she was going to die. She managed to dial the hotline number. The phone was busy. She tried again. And again. On the third attempt, she finally got through. A gracious sounding voice answered, "Poison control hotline, please hold." My sister-in-law was too shocked to speak. She thought she was dying of ptomaine poisoning, and they put her on hold. In her hour of great need, there was no one there to respond.

Is this how many of your young people feel about God? Do they think that He's too busy to care about them? That He doesn't really want to relate or talk to them? That He's aloof and uncaring about their deepest needs? As spiritual leaders, we want to communicate to kids that God both cares and desires to communicate with them. They can build a relationship with Him that lasts. They can stay connected with God and His purposes.

Identify the Condition of Your Group Members

How do your kids feel about their relationship with God? In most youth groups, kids' opinions vary widely. A few might feel that Jesus walks with them as their best friend, while others sense that their relationship with God either does not exist or has been put "on hold"—with no communication either way.

How do we find out what group members think so that we can make sure we address the *real* needs of our kids? A formal or informal survey serves as an excellent starting point. A survey or personal conversation helps us discover if kids ever read the Bible on their own, pray for others, or serve others in a way that is consciously connected with their faith (some participate in good deeds without really connecting it as an outflow of their relationship with God).

A printed survey (or one-on-one conversations with group members) might include questions like the following:

1. What have you read lately in the Bible?

2. Do you feel that God speaks to you through the Bible? Through prayer?

3. When do you feel most connected to God?

4. What do these terms mean to you: prayer, worship, fellowship?

5. What are some examples of service that you think a junior higher could attempt? Have you ever tried any of these?

6. What do you think are your greatest obstacles to reading the Bible? To prayer? To serving others?

7. Do you believe that God really loves you and wants to communicate with you?

The answers to these questions help us understand the spiritual perspectives of group members. This in turn equips us to adapt and utilize the sessions that follow in order to fit the needs we uncover.

Find Out What's Working and Build on It

Another step—perhaps again achieved through some formal research like a survey, although informal conversations usually yield better results—is to find out what positively affects kids regarding the Bible, prayer, fellowship, worship, and serving.

What aspects of worship seem to have the greatest impact on them? Why do some kids pray while others do not? Is there an effective way already in place that involves kids in Bible study? If kids are serving, what attracts them to service and how are they growing as a result?

Discovering the answers to these questions gives us concrete ideas to build on. We need not create new programs or devise new tactics if something already works in the lives of young people. As we encourage increased Scripture study, prayer, worship, fellowship, and service, we can build on models we observe in junior highers who exemplify what we want to stimulate in the whole group.

A young person involved in care for the handicapped or in outreach at a nursing home illustrates an example of service. Kids who already write in a journal as part of their prayer time and Bible study can share their experiences with the whole group. Group members who lead in prayer or worship demonstrate some of the growth possibilities for others in the group.

Steps toward Greater Effectiveness

Our goal is to help kids connect with God, to sense that He communicates with them and desires to be involved in their daily lives. As you use the sessions in this book, keep the following principles in mind.

• *Be realistic.* Try not to overload kids with unrealistic expectations about what spirituality looks like. Spiritual growth does not require pious language and sanctimonious behavior. We want to help kids grow as followers of Jesus Christ, not become thirteen-year-old Pharisees who use spiritual pretense to mask a judgmental spirit of others.

We once had a young person in the youth group who started getting very excited about his spiritual growth. Unfortunately, genuine spiritual growth started degenerating due to the influence of some well-meaning, pietistic adults. The young man started talking in King James English, praying with words like "Verily" and "multitudinous blessings" and using only "Thee," "Thou," and "Thy" in reference to God. The issue came to a head when he began "smiting sinners" at school with his enormous black leather Bible.

Highly influenceable young people respond to the expectations we thrust upon them, so let's make sure we dedicate ourselves to helping our kids "connect" with God in ways that positively affect their growth.

• *Meet them on their level.* Talk in terms kids understand. The writings of Richard Foster or the classical work of Bernard of Clairvaux may be changing your life spiritually, but make sure to translate what you're learning into language a teenager can understand.

• *Exemplify what you teach.* As we lead, we can feel free to make sure that kids understand our difficulties in "staying connected" with God. Young people do not expect us to be perfect, but they often think that being "spiritual" is easier for adults: "Of course you write in a journal; you're old!"

Kids need to know our struggles because sharing them helps the young people realize that their problems are normal. However, kids also need to know that we strive to do what we teach. Therefore, we should be writing in our journals and showing kids how we do it. I periodically ask kids to hold me accountable regarding prayer. When we lead the group in worship, we set the pact with our own worship. In group functions, we can demonstrate the difference between fellowship and simply having fun together. If we look for opportunities to serve, we imitate Jesus and Paul by leading with the imperative, "Follow me."

• *Adjust your schedule accordingly.* To implement these sessions, we need to allow time in the overall youth program. The activity-orientation of most youth groups often precludes any time allotment to help kids stay connected with God. Kids doubt the priority of worship, serving, or fellowship if there is no impact on the youth group schedule.

To encourage Bible study and prayer, we should allow time on a retreat for daily personal Bible study, writing in journals, and personal worship. We can factor corporate worship and fellowship time into weekly activities like Sunday school or mid-week Bible study. If we build service opportunities into the youth group calendar, kids are more likely to take action.

Two years ago, Jim cut back on his youth group "fun" activities because he saw that there were no opportunities for group members to engage in significant service to others, and the schedule was too full to add anything else. At first, kids (and some parents) complained because the monthly "fun" activities were reduced from four to three. Jim weathered the complaints and endured. After several months, kids (and some parents) began recommending more service opportunities because they could see the growth in their lives. But these results occurred because Jim wanted a schedule that reflected his real priorities for the group.

Francis Schaeffer wrote a book titled *God Is There and He Is Not Silent.* This is the message that we desire to communicate to young people. God does not put us on hold or neglect us in our moments of need. He desires to commune and communicate with us. We can stay connected with God because He desires to stay connected with us.

Paul Borthwick is minister of missions at Grace Chapel in Lexington, Massachusetts. A former youth pastor and frequent speaker to youth workers, he is author of several books including Organizing Your Youth Ministry *and* Feeding Your Forgotten Soul: Spiritual Growth for Youth Workers *(Zondervan).*

The images on these two pages are designed to help you promote this course within your church and community. Feel free to photocopy anything here and adapt it to fit your publicity needs. The stuff on this page could be used as a flier that you send or hand out to kids—or as a bulletin insert. The stuff on the next page could be used to add visual interest to newsletters, calendars, bulletin boards, or other promotions. Be creative and have fun!

How's Your Relationship with God?

Is reading the Bible a chore for you? Do you ever fall asleep in the middle of your prayer time? Does God seem a little more "distant" than you'd like Him to be? In our new series *Extreme Closeup,* we'll explore some practical ways for you to improve your relationship with the Lord. If you'd like some helpful tips on reading the Bible, praying, and serving others, join us.

Who:

When:

Where:

Questions? Call:

Extreme Closeup

Extreme Closeup

Are you "on line" with God?

We can't tell you what's going
to happen in our next meeting.

Make a joyful noise.

1 Why Read the Bible?

To James from God

Choose   one   or   more

☐ To help kids discover that the Bible is an interesting book that can be enjoyable and beneficial to them.

☐ To help kids understand that the Bible is God's "love letter" to us.

☐ To help kids establish a daily time in the Bible that will strengthen their relationship with God.

☐ Other _____

_____

Your Bible Base:

Psalms 1; 119:97-105

Love Letters

(Needed: Table, paper, pencils, envelopes, stamps, wastebasket, chalkboard and chalk or newsprint and marker, prizes)

Have kids form teams of three. Explain that they will be competing in a "love letter relay." Instruct the teams to stand at one end of the room in single-file lines. At the opposite end of the room, set up a long table. Place a piece of paper, a pencil, an envelope, and a stamp together in a pile on the table for each team. Explain that each team must write a love letter, fold it up, put it in the envelope, seal the envelope, address it, stamp it, and then drop it in the "mailbox" (a wastebasket that you've set up on the opposite end of the room from the table).

Each of the three team members will perform two steps of the process. After the first person from each team has finished his or her first assignment, he or she must run back to tag the next team member, who will then complete his or her assignment, and so on. Each team will go through the line twice.

The six steps of the process are as follows (write them on the board so that contestants will know exactly what to do):

1—Write "My Dearest [the name of a person in the group], I love you so much. I want you to love me, so let me tell you a little bit about myself."

2—Write "My favorite food is _____. My favorite TV show is _____. My favorite music group is _____."

3—Write "Would you like to get to know me better? Circle yes or no. Love, [your name]."

4—Fold the letter, put it in the envelope, and seal the envelope.

5—Address the envelope to [the name of a person in the group], [the name and address of your church]. Use your own address for the return address. Then put a stamp on the envelope.

6—Drop the letter off in the "mailbox," run back to your team, and sit down.

The first team to get its letter dropped off in the mailbox and then have everyone on the team sitting in a single-file line is the winner. Afterward, open the letter of the winning team to make sure that everything was done correctly. Then award prizes to the winning team members.

Unopened Mail

Say: **Wow, if I'd known that writing love letters was that much trouble, I never would have written the thousands I wrote when I was in junior high!**

After your kids stop hooting and hollering over your "slight exaggeration," ask: **How would you feel if someone sent you a love letter?** (Flattered, eager to read what it says, curious, overjoyed, embarrassed.)

If you came home from school one day and found a letter in the mail addressed to you, how long would you wait before opening it? Why? (Most kids probably wouldn't wait very long because receiving a letter is exciting.)

Point out that God has sent us a letter—a *love* letter, no less—called the Bible. In this letter, God tells us how much He loves us. He also tells us a lot about Himself—through actual events that happened in history, through parables, and especially through His Son, Jesus Christ.

Explain to your kids that for a variety of reasons, people often treat the Bible like an unopened piece of mail, never bothering to check what's inside. That's too bad, because they're missing out on some very interesting reading material.

Blockbuster Bible

(Needed: Bibles, copies of Repro Resource 1, pencils, prizes [optional])

Have kids form groups of three or four. Hand out copies of "Bible Epics" (Repro Resource 1) and pencils to each group. You might want to give the following references for the Bible stories listed on the sheet: *David and Bathsheba*—II Samuel 11:1–12:25; *Jacob and Esau*—Genesis 25:21-34; 27:1–33:20; *Esther*—Esther 1–9; *the birth of Jesus*—Matthew 1:18–2:23; Luke 1:26–2:40. Give the groups a few minutes to fill out the

sheet. When everyone is finished, have a spokesperson for each group read what his or her group came up with for movie titles, actors and actresses to star in the movies, and movie categories. Vote to see which group came up with the most clever movie title and which group came up with the best casting for actors and actresses. Award prizes, if you like.

Afterward, say: **We've seen that the Bible is more than just genealogies in which someone "begat" somebody else or weird laws like prohibiting cutting the hair on the side of your head or clipping off the edges of your beard** (Leviticus 19:27)**. The Bible also teaches us how God wants us to live and gives us answers on how we and God can become better connected. Let's take a look.**

STEP
4

What's in It for Me?

(Needed: Bibles, dictionary, stopwatch, blindfold)

Have kids turn in their Bibles to Psalm 1. Ask for a volunteer to read aloud the psalm. Afterward, ask: **What do you think it means to be blessed?** (Kids may offer such answers as "to receive some special favor" or "to be lucky.")

After a few kids have responded, pull out your trusty *Webster's New Collegiate Dictionary* and read what "blessed" really means—"of or enjoying happiness." Then ask: **Based on this meaning of "blessed," what are some words that people today might substitute for "blessed" in Psalm 1:1?** (Rich, well-liked, popular, successful, etc.) Explain that even though it's tempting to enjoy material, worldly things in our lives, we shouldn't let them become our main focus because they won't make us blessed.

Have your volunteer read Psalm 1:2 again. Then say: **Verse 2 indicates that this "blessed" person whom the writer is talking about isn't focusing on some of those material things we've just mentioned. It says his delight is in the law of the Lord and that He meditates on that law day and night. What is the law of the Lord?** (His Word, the Bible.)

Your kids may not be too sold on the idea of being "in the Bible" for more than a few minutes, not to mention being in it "day and night." Ask them the following questions to lighten the mood: **What's the** latest you've ever stayed up studying for a test or doing homework? Have you ever stayed up all night before? If so, when? Get several responses.

Explain to your kids that Psalm 1:2 isn't talking about twenty-four-hour Bible vigils; it's talking about reading and studying God's Word enough so that its teachings constantly "shine through" in our everyday lives.

Highlight the benefits of delighting in God's Word by having kids find God's promises to us in verses 3 ("whatever he does prospers") and 6 ("the Lord watches over the way of the righteous").

Have your kids turn to Psalm 119. Ask for a volunteer to read aloud verses 97-105. Then ask: **How would you describe the attitude of this psalm's writer, based on verses 97-104?** (Confident, because he knows that meditating on God's laws makes him wiser than other people, particularly his enemies; happy, almost giddy, about God's law in verses 97 and 103.)

How would you describe your attitude when you think about God's law and what the Bible has to say? Explain that we should delight in reading God's Word, rather than approaching it negatively, assuming that the Bible simply tells us what we *can't* do.

Emphasize that God's Word can be a lamp to our feet and a light to our path. Then ask: **When might the Bible be a light in your life?** (When you feel lonely, when you're unsure about what to do, when you struggle with temptation, when you don't feel joy, despite the fact that you're a Christian.)

Ask two kids to leave the room. Have the rest of the group members set up a maze in your meeting room (using pathways of chairs, desks, etc.) that the two volunteers will have to maneuver through by crawling. When the maze is set up, have the volunteers come in one at a time. Blindfold one of them. Have each of them crawl through the maze, timing each one with a stopwatch to see who gets through the maze the quickest.

Afterward (assuming the blindfolded contestant lost the race), ask: **What might have helped** [name of blindfolded contestant] **get through the maze quicker? How might you compare reading and studying God's Word with the maze activity we just did?** (Studying God's Word makes navigating the "maze" of life a bit easier by giving us light for our path and a lamp for our feet.)

STEP 5

Take Hold of the Wheel!

(Needed: Two chairs)

Say: **For those of you who haven't driven before, how do you feel when you think about finally getting to drive?** (Scared, excited, nervous, pumped up, unsure, confident, etc.)

How would you feel if, during your entire driver's education class, you never once got to drive, not even around the parking lot? Explain that in case this unfortunate circumstance should ever happen to any of your group members, you're going to give them a simulated driving experience to see if they would be up to the test.

Ask for a volunteer to come to the front of the room. Set two chairs next to each other at the front of the room to serve as the driver's and passenger's seats of a driver's ed car. Announce that you will serve as the instructor.

Explain to your volunteer and to the other group members that the volunteer is to pretend that he or she is backing out of a driveway and then pulling away. Let your kids know that you have a list of the actual steps that must take place for this driving manuever to be done successfully. Explain that whenever the volunteer misses a step or makes a mistake, you will say, **You forgot something** or **Are you sure you want to do that?** The volunteer must then figure out what he or she did wrong. If the volunteer can't figure it out, check to see if any of the other group members know.

The proper steps are as follows:

(1) Open the door.

(2) Sit in the driver's seat.

(3) Close the door.

(4) Fasten your seatbelt.

(5) Adjust mirrors.

(6) Lock doors.

(7) Put the key in the ignition to start the car.

(8) Place your hands on the steering wheel in the "10 and 2" position.

(9) Press down on the brake pedal and put the car in reverse.

(10) Press slightly on the brake pedal, with your left hand on the steering wheel and your right hand on the back of passenger seat as you turn to look behind you over your right shoulder.

(11) Let off the brake slightly to move down the driveway, but brake

at the edge of driveway, checking both ways for cars.

(12) Press the gas pedal enough to back out into your lane of traffic, as you turn the steering wheel to get into your lane.

(13) Brake.

(14) Put the car into drive and turn the steering wheel back in the opposite direction to compensate for the turn you made to get into your lane.

(15) Press on the gas pedal to take off down the road.

Afterward, applaud the volunteer for his or her participation. Then ask: **How might we relate the example of being in driver's ed—but never driving—to studying God's Word?** (It doesn't matter much if you've just *heard* about what God's Word says without having any personal, "hands on" experience with it.)

Ask kids to reflect on these questions: **Do you need to "get behind the wheel of God's Word" yourself? If so, how can you go about it?**

STEP
6

Baby Steps

(Needed: Copies of Repro Resource 2, pencils)

Ask: **If you wanted to become a world-class runner, what might be some steps you would take to achieve that goal?** (Kids may mention things like training, running every day, getting good shoes, stretching, etc.)

If no one mentions it, ask: **How about learning to run?** Then ask what steps they would need to take to learn to run. If no one mentions it, ask: **How about learning to walk?** Kids should pick up on the pattern as you progress downwardly to standing, crawling, and learning balance.

The point you're trying to make is that we need to take "baby steps" to gradually progress to the point where we can begin to take bigger and bigger steps. The same principle holds true when it comes to studying God's Word.

Explain that you're not expecting group members to have the Old Testament read and outlined by next week's meeting. Instead, emphasize that setting *and meeting* small goals of consistently being in God's Word can help lay a strong foundation of being connected with God.

Don't restrict kids with a certain Bible-study format. Instead, encour-

age them to decide what steps *they* want to take in areas such as
- choosing a time to be in God's Word
- choosing a book or passage of the Bible to study
- choosing a translation of the Bible they're comfortable with
- choosing a devotional guide they enjoy
- choosing a setting in which they will have their study time.

Hand out copies of "Baby-Stepping through the Bible," (Repro Resource 2). After kids have read through the instructions, answer any questions they may have about the activity. After a few minutes, close the session in prayer, asking God to help the Bible come alive for your group members.

BIBLE EPICS

You're a film producer in Hollywood. After watching *The Ten Commandments* on TV, you decide that Hollywood should be making more movies based on Bible stories. Below is a list of some Bible stories that might have potential as movies. Your job is to come up with a title for each movie, decide who would play the major roles, and determine what type of movie (comedy, action-adventure, romance, etc.) you'll make from each Bible story. We've left one spot blank for you to come up with your own Bible story to film.

Bible Story	Movie Title	Stars	Movie Category
David and Bathsheba			
Jacob and Esau			
Esther			
The birth of Jesus			

Baby-Stepping through the Bible

Do you think you can set aside 10-15 minutes a day to read the Bible? Let's see. Write today's date in the upper left-hand box. Then write in the dates of the next 27 days following today, which will give you four full weeks. For each day that you spend at least 10-15 minutes reading the Bible, write in that square what passage(s) you read. If you don't have a Bible study time, draw an "X" through that day. After 28 days, bring in your calendar and be prepared to discuss any impact that the last four weeks have had in your relationship with God.

Step 4

At the beginning of the step, make sure that each person has a Bible. Bring out an ample supply of string, masking tape, and bendable metal coat hangers. Challenge kids to use these materials to make "Bible holders" that keep their Bibles open and in front of them (without requiring the use of hands or tables) during this step. Then discuss where kids usually keep their Bibles. Ask: **How close at hand should our Bibles be? Why?**

Step 6

Stage a bread-eating contest. One team gets a large, unsliced loaf of hard-crusted bread; the other team gets a plateful of cut-up, bite-sized pieces. Neither team may use its hands. After one minute, see how much progress each team has made. Discuss the fact that it's much easier to "eat" the Bible a bit at a time instead of diving in and trying to consume it in huge chunks.

Step 1

With a small group, you might want to try a different opener. Have kids form two teams. Give each team a stack of magazines, scissors, paper, and tape or glue. Explain that the teams will be competing to see which can create a love note first by cutting out letters and words from the magazines and taping or gluing them on the sheet of paper (ransom-note style). The first team to create a complete love note is the winner.

Step 6

In connection with the commitment requested from your group members on Repro Resource 2, let kids know that small groups have opportunities larger groups don't. For example, depending on your own willingness, you might say: **If you are doing individual Bible reading during the week and happen upon a particularly noteworthy or interesting passage, give me a call. If you think that what you've found is important, perhaps everyone else will too. We can try to study it as a group.** Naturally you won't be able to do this if everyone calls with a different passage. But as kids begin to connect what they're doing on their own with what they're doing at your weekly group meetings, they are likely to get a lot more meaning out of God's "love letter."

Step 3

Give your group members an opportunity to use their creativity a little more by having them create sequels to the "movies" they described on Repro Resource 1. After the members of each group have shared their resonses, ask them to choose one of the Bible stories to do a follow-up to. Instruct the groups to create a "trailer" (a preview) for their sequel. (For example, "First he lost his birthright. Then he lost his blessing. This time, Esau's going to win—at any cost. Coming this summer—*Birthright II: The Wrath of Esau.*") After a few minutes, have each group share what it came up with. Then lead in to Step 4.

Step 6

As you wrap up the session, help your group members recognize that reading the Bible doesn't have to be a chore. Point out that there are some pretty interesting stories in God's Word. Have kids form groups. Instruct the members of each group to write headlines for Bible stories as they might appear on the front page of a supermarket tabloid. (For example, the headline for a story about Noah might read "Man Claiming End of World Is Near Builds Giant Floating Zoo.") Have each group choose two or three stories to work on. After a few minutes, have each group share its headlines. Emphasize that while not all Bible passages are "exciting," your kids may be surprised at how interesting many portions are.

Step 2

Describing the Bible as a love letter isn't a new analogy—and if kids have heard it before, they may have had time to consider whether it really makes sense. What kind of love letter is thousands of pages long, spends much of its time on history and rules, comes from an invisible sender, and doesn't have the recipient's name on it? Don't count on this analogy to make kids eager to read the Bible; instead, include it as only one of several comparisons. Ask kids to come up with their own. For example, the Bible is also like a car owner's manual, a computer database, a cookbook, a time machine, a diary, and a novel. Yet it's like no other book—which is still another reason to read it.

Step 6

If your kids are experienced churchgoers, they've probably heard repeated admonitions to read the Bible. Perhaps they've even tried it—and given up. Chances are that the Repro Resource 2 take-home activity will be ignored. Instead, consider one of these alternatives: (1) asking kids to try 1-5 minutes a day rather than 10-15, or three times a week instead of daily; (2) using part of your next meeting as a time for kids to practice individual Bible reading under your supervision; (3) pairing volunteers to have "telephone devotions" once or twice this week, taking turns reading a Bible passage to each other and then discussing it.

Step 3

Group members who are not familiar with the Bible may not know all of the stories referred to on Repro Resource 1. So rather than handing out the sheet, you might want to talk kids through the exercise. (Besides, creative ideas usually flow better in a group setting, rather than an individual setting.) Depending on the knowledge of your group members, you might want to substitute "David and Goliath" for "David and Bathsheba," "Cain and Abel" for "Jacob and Esau," and "Jonah" for "Esther." Another option is to use actual movie titles and then try to think of Bible stories that they might describe. For instance, *The Lion King* could be about Daniel; *The River Wild* could be about the baby Moses; *The Nightmare before Christmas* could be about Herod's killing of the innocent children; and so forth.

Step 4

In connection with your study of Psalm 1, bring in something to plant. (The easiest thing might be bulbs that come packaged with their own vases, available at most nature shops and elsewhere.) When you discuss "a tree planted by streams of water," pull out your plant and explain that you're going to plant it to see what happens. As the plant grows over the next few weeks and months, kids should be reminded of the importance of their own spiritual growth. (Just be sure to remove the plant in its prime, before it withers and dies.)

Step 1

As kids arrive, hand them paper and pencils. To begin the session, instruct kids to complete the following statements:
• The best book I've ever read is . . .
• I really liked that book because . . .
• The reason I read it is . . .
• I would/would not recommend it to my friends because . . .

After a few minutes, have kids mill around the room, sharing their answers. Any who have chosen the same book should congregate together. After a few minutes of mingling, ask kids to share their answers. Point out that kids who chose the same book probably have different reasons for choosing it. If no one chose the Bible, ask why not. (Chances are pretty good that kids will say it's boring and that they don't understand it.) Explain that over the next few weeks, you'll be taking an extreme close-up look at the Bible. Suggest that your kids may discover that it's anything but boring, and that there are ways to help us understand it.

Step 6

Bring in a recording of Amy Grant's song "Thy Word." Before playing it, however, make sure that each person has a sheet of paper and a pencil. As kids listen to the song, have them write down the ways that God's Word helps us, as mentioned in the song. After the song is over, encourage kids to share their lists. As they share, make a "master list" on the board that everyone can see. Then play the song again. While the song is playing this time, encourage kids to thank God for all He's given us through His Word.

Step 4

After talking about the fact that the Bible is a lamp to our feet, hand out paper and pencils. Explain that you want to help your group members see how the Bible can help them with the problems they face every day. Ask your girls to think about a problem they or someone they know is facing right now that might require an answer from the Bible. Have them write it down. Emphasize that they don't need to write their names on the sheet. Assure them that no problem is too large or too small for God's love and attention. Collect the papers and briefly read through them. If there are any problems that you can respond to with Scripture, do so immediately. If not, explain that you'll look the sheets over this week and bring them back to discuss the following week. As you're looking for answers, try to find references that are story examples or that are as close to the problem as possible. Kids know when they're getting general, "pat" answers. Bring their questions and your answers back next week. It's important to follow through on this activity.

Step 6

If possible, take a few minutes to visit your church's nursery, encouraging your girls to notice all they can about the babies—the noises they make, their physical capabilities, their ability to do things for themselves, etc. After a few minutes, return to your own room to share your findings. Ask: **What would happen if a baby never grew?** You may or may not get responses to this question. Then say: **God designed us to start out small and then to grow. That's how He designed us spiritually as well. We may need to start by doing "baby" things, but He wants us to continue to grow. The way we do that is by reading His Word.** Go through Repro Resource 2 as instructed in the session.

Step 1

Rework the relay exercise so that team members write portions of the letter for the last person on the team to read and follow to find an edible prize. For example, adapt the following instructions for your own church: "(1) Dear Group Member— Go down the stairs; (2) Turn left and go down the hall; (3) At the end of the hall, turn right and go to the second room on the left; (4) Enter the room and turn on the lights; (5) You'll find a special treat in the refrigerator. Love, Your Youth Leader." Make a copy of these instructions for each team. Place each numbered step in an individual envelope. The first person on each team should run across the room, pick up one of the envelopes marked "#1," open it, and begin a letter by writing (on stationery that you've provided) what's on the instructions. Then he should return to his team and tag the second person, who will run to open the second envelope and add to the letter. After the fifth person finishes, the sixth person should run to the letter, grab it, and follow the instructions.

Step 2

Most guys like to get mail as much as girls do; but in many cases, girls seem to do a much better job of responding. Challenge your guys to acknowledge gifts from other people. When given gifts, they should write thank-you notes. When they get letters, they should write back. And when they realize that God's Word is like a personal letter for their own benefit and encouragement, they should not only read it, but respond to it as well. Ask: **How should you respond to a letter that God has written?** (Doing what it says shows respect. Praying is a way of "writing back" and letting God know *our* thoughts. Being decent to other people is equated to treating God well [see Matthew 25:31-46].)

Step 4

If possible, meet in an extremely dark area to do the Bible study portion of the session. The ideal place will have just *barely* enough light to see to read. Or you might meet in a completely dark room with a penlight as your only source of light. As you study Psalm 1, no one will understand what's going on. But when your volunteer reader gets to Psalm 119:105, arrange for someone to hit the light switch. Flood the room with as much light as possible. Then spend a few minutes discussing how the Bible can make a similar change in the lives of your young people.

Step 6

Hand out paper and pencils. Ask kids to write out a number of specific instructions using the following formula: "If you want to learn to _____, you need to _____." Use the driving instructions in Step 5 as an example. The instructions don't have to be quite that detailed, but they should be very specific. Instruct kids to write the "If you want to learn to" statement at the top of the sheet and the instructions at the bottom of the sheet. Kids may write down as many ideas as they wish (on separate sheets of paper). Examples might include how to tie your shoe, kiss somebody, siphon gas out of a car, kick a field goal, drink out of a straw, blow your nose, or whatever. After a few minutes, collect the sheets. Cut apart the top section of each sheet from the bottom one. Then look for unusual "matches" where the instructions make for a humorous conclusion to the opening statement. Use this activity to lead in to the "If you want to learn to run" discussion.

Step 3

Show scenes (after pre-screening them for appropriateness) from some of the following videos. Then discuss, using the questions provided. During discussion, note that the Bible contains a lot more than family trees and rules.

• *Ace Ventura, Pet Detective.* Play a scene in which Ace (Jim Carrey) acts especially goofy and out-of-control. Ask: **Can you think of someone in the Bible who acted crazy or weird?** (David pretended to be crazy [I Samuel 21]; Nebuchadnezzar went temporarily insane and acted like an animal [Daniel 4].)

• *Tombstone.* Play a scene from the showdown at the OK Corral. Ask: **What are some showdowns you remember from the Bible?** (David vs. Goliath [I Samuel 17]; Peter vs. the soldier in the Garden of Gethsemane [Matthew 26].)

• *The Adventures of Baron Munchausen.* Show one of the many scenes using impressive special effects. Ask: **What are some Bible events that would require special effects to show on the screen?** (Any of the miracles; most of the Book of Revelation.)

• *Jurassic Park.* Show a scene featuring one or more of the largest dinosaurs. Ask: **Can you think of any large or unusual creatures mentioned in the Bible?** (The great fish that swallowed Jonah [Jonah 1]; the creatures around God's throne in heaven [Revelation 4].)

Step 4

Play and discuss one or more contemporary Christian songs that encourage Bible reading. Some examples might include "End of the Book" (Michael W. Smith), "Thy Word" (Amy Grant), "The More I Know of You" (Glad), and "He'll Shine His Light on You" (Michelle Pillar).

Step 1

Replace Steps 1 and 2 with a shorter opener. Wrap three pocket New Testaments in gift wrap; tape a "#1" tag to each one. Also wrap three boxes of Milk Duds, Junior Mints, or other candy; tape a "#2" tag to each one. Have three volunteers come to the front of the room and choose between package #1 and package #2. Let volunteers unwrap their choices at the same time. Discuss who got the best "deals" and why.

Step 3

In place of Repro Resource 1, have each group choose a Bible character (or assign one to each group). Instruct each group to come up with a hypothetical telephone answering machine message for that person. The message should include the character's name, two things he or she might be doing instead of answering the phone, and a unique "sound" after which the caller is to leave a message. (For example: "Hi. This is Daniel. I can't come to the phone right now because I'm eating my vegetables—or because I'm having a vision about a guy made out of different kinds of metal. Please leave a message after the lion's roar.") Have kids read (or tape and play) the results; then discuss the Bible stories referred to in the messages. In Step 4, skip the maze activity. Skip Step 5 too.

Step 1

You'll need to bring in a stopwatch and sixty-six books of varying sizes and shapes. Stack the books at one end of your meeting area. To begin the session, have kids form two teams. Instruct the members of one team to line up at the opposite end of the room from the books. See how long it takes the team to transport (relay-style) the books from one end of the room to the other. The first person in line will run to other side of the room, grab a book, run back to his or her team, set the book down, and tag the next person in line. That person will then do the same thing. The team will continue until all sixty-six books have been moved. Write the first team's time on the board; then see if the second team can better it. After the game, see if your group members can guess the topic of the session based on the clue of "sixty-six books." (There are sixty-six books in the Bible.)

Step 3

After you've gone through Repro Resource 1, help your group members see that the Bible contains stories that are relevant to kids today. Have kids read Genesis 16:1-16; 21:8-21, in which God provides for Hagar—a single mother—and her son Ishmael. Then ask: **Do you think God still takes care of single parents and their families today? If so, how?**

COMBINED

Step 3

For the Repro Resource 1 activity, divide kids into groups of three or four, making sure that you mix your junior highers and high schoolers. After kids have completed Repro Resource 1, give them the Scripture references for the stories listed on the sheet. Instruct the groups to look up the references and identify the principle (or principles) shown in each passage that God wants us to follow. Also ask the groups to identify ways shown in each passage that we and God can become better connected. After a few minutes, have each group share what it came up with.

Step 4

Instead of asking only two kids to leave the room, dismiss all of your junior highers (with a lot of supervision, of course). Then have your high schoolers set up the maze that the junior highers will have to crawl through. As your high schoolers are setting up the maze, have them identify problems and obstacles they faced when they were in junior high and how a better knowledge of God's Word would have helped them. Then call in your junior highers to crawl through the maze, blindfolding some but not others. After all of them have gone through the maze, discuss the ways in which life is similar to the maze. Then call for high school volunteers to share the obstacles and dead-ends they hit when they were in junior high.

SIXTH GRADE

Step 3

Briefly review each of the stories on Repro Resource 1. As you're reviewing each story, make some kind of a "mistake" in your retelling. See how many kids correct you. (For instance, you might say: **Esau sold his birthright to his brother Jacob for $500.**) In addition to being fun for your kids, this exercise should give you an idea of your group members' biblical literacy. If your group members don't catch one of your mistakes, be sure to correct it yourself. After all, the last thing you want to do is arm kids with false information about the Bible!

Step 6

Describe—but don't let kids taste—a plateful of individually wrapped treats. Tie this into the need to "taste" Scripture for ourselves. Hand out Repro Resource 2 along with the wrapped treats, asking kids to save the treats until they've first "tasted" at least one Bible verse at home.

PLANNING CHECKLIST

Date Used:

Approx.
Time

Step 1: Love Lettes _____
o Small Group
o Fellowship & Worship
o Mostly Guys
o Short Meeting Time
o Urban
Things needed:

Step 2: Unopened Mail _____
o Heard It All Before
o Mostly Guys
Things needed:

Step 3: Blockbuster Bible _____
o Large Group
o Little Bible Background
o Media
o Short Meeting Time
o Urban
o Combined Junior High/High School
o Sixth Grade
Things needed:

**Step 4: What's in It
for Me?** _____
o Extra Action
o Little Bible Background
o Mostly Girls
o Extra Fun
o Media
o Combined Junior High/High School
Things needed:

**Step 5: Take Hold of the
Wheel!** _____
Things needed:

Step 6: Baby Steps _____
o Extra Action
o Small Group
o Large Group
o Heard It All Before
o Fellowship & Worship
o Mostly Girls
o Extra Fun
o Sixth Grade
Things needed:

"HEAVEN NET"
LORD, THANK YOU FOR HELPING ME SOLVE THAT PROBLEM WITH MOM. I NEVER COULD HAVE DONE IT WITHOUT YOU. YOU'RE ALWAYS THERE WHEN I NEED YOU.

YOUR GOALS FOR THIS SESSION:

Choose one or more

☐ To help kids recognize that God wants to communicate with us.

☐ To help kids understand that communicating with God involves both talking and listening.

☐ To encourage kids to develop the daily discipline of prayer in their own lives, perhaps using a written journal.

☐ Other _____
_____

Your Bible Base:

II Chronicles 7:14
Matthew 6:5-8; 7:7-11

O P T I O N S

EXTRA ACTION

LARGE GROUP

FELLOWSHIP & WORSHIP

MOSTLY GIRLS

EXTRA FUN

MEDIA

SHORT MEETING TIME

SIXTH GRADE

STEP 1

Let Me Finish!

(Needed: Copies of Repro Resource 3, pencils, prize)

Hand out copies of "Hitting the Cutoff Man" (Repro Resource 3) and pencils. If kids don't understand the instructions on the sheet, explain that this is a race to see who can connect all of the pairs of connected comments the quickest. When someone completes his or her sheet, he or she should hand it to you. Wait until everyone has finished the sheet before discussing the correct answers. Then check the paper of the person who finished first. If his or her answers are correct, give him or her a prize. If the sheet wasn't totally correct, go to the sheet of the person who finished second and grade that paper. Continue in this manner until a winner is found. The answers for Repro Resource 3 are as follows: 1—f; 2—d; 3—j; 4—b; 5—a; 6—g; 7—c; 8—h; 9—e; 10—i.

STEP 2

It's a Two-Way Street

(Needed: Copies of Repro Resource 4)

Say: **We've just worked through some examples in which people were cut off by others. Now it's time to give you a chance to experience it for yourself.**

Ask for a couple of volunteers. Hand each of them a copy of "Zip the Lip!" (Repro Resource 4). Give your volunteers a few minutes to read through the scenario before they act it out in front of the group.

After the presentation, ask your kids to describe a time in their lives when they were cut off or interrupted while talking to someone. Encourage them to describe how they felt when this happened.

Ask: **When people interrupt someone who is speaking to add their own comments, what might that say to the person who was cut off?** (He or she is not being listened to. The other person thought of something important to say. The other person is rude.)

Say: **Let's think about prayer for a moment. What are some ways during prayer that we might make God feel like He is being "cut off"?** If no one mentions them, suggest things like not focusing on God during prayer and rattling off a list of things that we want from God without listening to what He might want to tell us through our consciences or thanking Him for all He's done for us.

Ask: **What are some other things that might keep us from having an effective prayer time with God?** Make a note of group members' responses so that you can address these problems later in the session.

Call-Waiting

(Needed: Bibles, chalkboard and chalk or newsprint and marker)

Ask: **How many of you have call-waiting on your telephone at home?** Ask some of the kids who have the service to share some reasons why they like it.

Then explain that call-waiting is similar to our "prayer line" to God. God has constant call-waiting. You can always get through to Him when you need to talk to Him; He's never busy.

Have someone read aloud II Chronicles 7:14. Then ask group members to think of a time when they prayed to God about something, but felt like God didn't answer their prayers.

Ask: **How did you feel when God didn't seem to be answering your prayers?** (Like He wasn't listening; like He doesn't care enough to pay attention.)

How might II Chronicles 7:14 change our thinking about God's answering people's prayers? If no one mentions it, point out that the verse doesn't say that if we just *pray*, God will hear us from heaven. It says that we are to be humble before God, seek Him, and turn from our wicked ways. In other words, we shouldn't pray to God for things while we are willingly living ungodly lives.

Write the following questions on the board for your kids to discuss:
• What is prayer?
• How should we pray?
• When and where are we supposed to pray?

• Is prayer better individually or in a group? Why?

After briefly discussing each of these questions, have volunteers read aloud Matthew 7:7-11 and Matthew 6:5-8. Then go through the questions on the board again, in light of these two passages.

Say: **Matthew 6:8 says that God knows what we need before we ask Him. So why should we pray when He already knows what we're going to say?** Let your kids wrestle with this question for a while. Then explain that God wants us to come to the realization that praying to Him can be a real power source in our lives. God knows the power He has and the blessings He wants to pour out on us when we pray to Him. And although we can be told by others that there's power in prayer, we won't *know* that until we experience it for ourselves.

Suggest that praying to God, who already knows what's on our hearts and minds, can be a bit unnerving at times. Ask: **Have you ever felt overwhelmed or in awe when you were praying to God? If so, explain. If not, why do you suppose that is?**

How do you think God feels when we have an attitude of awe toward Him? Explain.

STEP 4

Write It Down!

(Needed: Chalkboard and chalk or newsprint and marker, prizes)

Ask for several volunteers to come to the front of the room. When they do, explain that they've been selected for a Bible spelling bee. Choose a few easy words for your kids to spell first; then move on to tougher words like Nebuchadnezzar and Thessalonians. If your volunteers are struggling a little bit, you might want to help them out a little. Award prizes for the top three finishers.

Afterward, ask: **After seeing what a spelling bee is like, how many of you would rather take a written spelling test?** Get a show of hands; then ask some of the kids who raised their hands why they would rather take a written test. Answers might include being nervous about having to talk out loud and being distracted in a public setting.

Relate the concept of a spelling bee to the idea of praying out loud to God. Point out that some people get nervous and distracted when they pray out loud.

Say: **If the idea of praying out loud sometimes rattles your**

OPTIONS

HEARD IT ALL BEFORE

MOSTLY GIRLS

MOSTLY GUYS

EXTRA FUN

JR. HIGH / HIGH SCHOOL COMBINED

SIXTH GRADE

prayer life, you might want to consider journaling. Explain that journaling is simply writing down what you want to say to God on a daily basis, as well as any insights and thoughts you have about areas of your life that you and God are working on.

Ask your kids to name some things that they think might make journaling hard for them. If no one mentions it, suggest that one concern might be writer's block (or, in this case, "journaling block")—not knowing what to write.

Explain that you've got a little formula that's a guaranteed cure for "journaling block"; it's called ACTS. Write the following four words on the board:

Adoration
Confession
Thanksgiving
Supplication

Explain that although these look like big words, they're simple in meaning, and can improve one's prayer life when used consistently. Discuss the four areas as a group, keeping in mind these four definitions:

Adoration—telling God how great He is
Confession—telling God things in your life that you're sorry for
Thanksgiving—telling God what you're thankful for
Supplication—telling God of any requests you might have

STEP
5

Personalizing Your Prayer Closet

Emphasize to your kids that journaling may not be for all of them. There are as many different styles of prayer as there are pray-ers. The point is that we shouldn't be worried if our spoken prayers don't rank up there with the polished prayers of pastors and evangelists. Read Matthew 6:5-8 again to remind your kids that God wants us to pray humbly before Him, not in a manner to impress others with our words.

As you wrap up the session, challenge kids to work on one specific area in their prayer lives that needs improvement. Maybe it's being "still before God" during prayer and listening more for what we might learn during that time. Or maybe it's getting in the habit of praying regularly to Him, or praying out loud in a group, or journaling our prayers to Him. Close the session by praying that your kids' prayer lives will be an area that connects them closer to God.

Draw connecting lines from the conversation starters on the left to the statements that cut them off on the right. Some are obvious and some aren't. Finish as quickly as possible, sign your name to your sheet, and hand it in to your leader.

CONVERSATION STARTERS

1. Did you watch *The Simpsons* last night? My favorite part was . . .

2. When I stepped outside this morning, I couldn't believe how humid it . . .

3. I'm getting really hungry. I feel like I could eat a . . .

4. Did you hear about Sue? I heard that yesterday after school . . .

5. Have you seen *Schindler's List*? I hear that . . .

6. Do you think the White Sox can win the World . . .

7. My parents are taking me shopping so I can pick out a present for my . . .

8. I'm excited about tomorrow's big game against South High, I can hardly . . .

9. I can't wait for the new Whitney Houston album to come out. It's supposed to be . . .

10. I'm thinking about signing up for the youth group's mission trip to . . .

INTERRUPTIONS

a. There's no way I could sit still for over three hours. I'm pretty squeamish too.

b. Have you noticed that she has alcohol on her breath all the time? I heard she was pretty messed up at her old school before coming here.

c. Hey, there's a mall-wide sale this weekend! Can you believe it?

d. I had to wring my shirt out after third period because I was sweating so much!

e. I hated *The Bodyguard.*

f. Oh, that Ned Flanders is so weird! I'd go crazy if he were my neighbor.

g. Who cares? Everybody knows that the Cubbies are the city's favorite team.

h. They've got a really great program. Haven't they been conference champs for the last three years?

i. Well, I'm kind of getting tired of going on Thursday nights. Power Hour isn't fun anymore, and lately, Pastor Donny has been way too boring.

j. Speaking of food, did you hear about the freshman who found a toenail in the chicken and dumplings they served for lunch today?

ZIP THE LIP!

Scene: Two teenagers are hanging out, shooting the breeze. The two have always been good friends, and haven't been able to talk to each other for a while. They are pretty excited about the opportunity to catch up on each other's lives.

FRIEND #1: Wow, it is so good to see you. We have—

FRIEND #2 *(cutting in)*: You know, we haven't talked in the longest time. It seems like forever. Oh, what were you saying?

FRIEND #1 *(laughing)*: Actually, I was just going to say the same thing, that we haven't talked in the longest time and that it seems like forever. Oh, I forgot to tell you that last weekend when you were out of town, a couple of friends and I went to see a movie. We saw—

FRIEND #2 *(excitedly interjecting)*: Oh, that reminds me—you've got to see the new movie *Betrayal of Friendship*! It was so suspenseful! I couldn't sleep at all the night I saw it! You'll love it! What did you see?

FRIEND #1 *(a bit deflated)*: Well, what I was *going* to tell you was that I saw the new movie *Betrayal of Friendship*, and that it was so suspenseful I couldn't sleep the night I saw it, and that I loved it.

FRIEND #2: Oh. Well, I guess we both loved it.

FRIEND #1: Yeah, I guess we did. *(Regaining excitement)* Anyway, do you have any plans this weekend? I thought we should maybe try out this new restaurant called—

FRIEND #2 *(nearly salivating while cutting in again)*: Oh, you'll die when you taste the food at this new restaurant I ate at. It's called "Straight from Heaven." Don't you just love the name? And the barbecued ribs there are soooo good! We've got to eat there. What's the place you want to eat at? I forgot what you said while I was thinking about those ribs!

FRIEND #1 *(a little peeved)*: I noticed. I guess it wouldn't be very exciting for you now. If you must know, I wanted to try out "Straight from Heaven." I just loved the name, and I heard that the barbecued ribs there were really good. But obviously, you just told me that.

FRIEND #2 *(half apologetically)*: I'm sorry. I just think of things that I want to say.

FRIEND #1 *(upset, yet composed)*: But you don't stop to think how rude it is to cut people off. It tells them that you're not really listening. Anyway, just work at it. Now, I've really got something to tell you. I was standing by my locker today when this really cute guy [or girl] walked up and—

FRIEND #2 *(absolutely ecstatic, cutting in)*: I almost forgot! Today during lunch, the cutest guy [or girl] came up to me and asked me out for Saturday night. He [or she] said I was the best-looking person in school. His [or her] name is Terry Taylor.

FRIEND #1 *(surprised)*: What? That's the same guy [or girl] that walked up to *me* at *my* locker today!

FRIEND #2: That can't be right! You're just jealous! What did he [or she] say to you?

FRIEND #1: Why should I tell you? I'm sure you know what I'm going to say anyway. Let's just say that you're not the only one with a date this weekend.

(Friend #2 storms out of the room.)

Step 1

Have kids form teams. Give each team a bag containing three paper cups, a ten-foot length of kite string, a candle, a rubber band, a toothpick, and a flashlight battery. Say: **In this bag, you have the makings of a working, two-way communication device. See whether you can make that device, using exactly five of the items, in three minutes. Go!** See what happens. The solution is to rub the candle on the string to thoroughly wax the string. Then use the toothpick to poke a hole in the bottom of each of two cups. Put the string through the holes; tie a large knot in each end of the string so that the string stays connected to the cups. Stretch the string taut. Two kids can talk and listen to each other as if the cups were telephones. Award a prize to each successful team, if you like. Use this activity to introduce the idea of low-tech, two-way communication.

Step 3

If you made paper-cup phones earlier (see the "Extra Action" option for Step 1), have partners try to read II Chronicles 7:14 to each other through their phones. Sound quality will be mediocre at best. Use this to lead into a discussion of what it feels like when our prayers don't seem to "connect" with God. In Step 4, bring four blocks of wood; write one of the four "ACTS" words on each block. Make the first letter of each word large and bold. Have kids form three teams. Give the first team fifteen seconds to stack the blocks so that the bold letters spell a word. Give the second team a chance to spell a different word; then give the third team a chance. (Possibilities include CATS, ACTS, and SCAT.) Discuss which arrangement of Adoration, Confession, Thanksgiving, and Supplication might make the best kind of prayer and why. Avoid insisting that kids follow the ACTS formula, however.

Step 3

Any time members of a small group discuss prayer, they should probably be reminded of Jesus' promise in Matthew 18:19, 20: "I tell you that if two of you on earth agree about anything you ask for, it will be done for you by my Father in heaven. For where two or three come together in my name, there am I with them." Emphasize that big numbers are not the secret to "big" prayer. The goal is for your group members to focus their thoughts and "come together." As they grow closer to Jesus as individuals, they will find themselves naturally pulling together as a group.

Step 5

Suggest that a small group is the best place to learn to pray out loud. As you conclude the session, challenge everyone to pray aloud—even if it's just one sentence. To reduce awkwardness for new people or for those unaccustomed to praying, ask each person to think of something specific to pray about. (It can be from any of the areas of adoration, confession, thanksgiving, or supplication.) When one person expresses a prayer request, find another person willing to pray about it during the closing prayer. Have your group members "trade off," with each person responsible for someone else's specific request. That gives everyone something to say. Anyone who wants to pray for things in addition to that specific request should feel free to do so. You should close the prayer session, filling in any "gaps" and thanking God for the opportunities He gives us to communicate with Him.

Step 1

Have kids form three teams. Give each team an Etch-a-Sketch. Before the session, you'll need to write a message (at least ten words long) on each team's Etch-a-Sketch; then cover each screen with a piece of paper so that no one else can see the message. Set up an obstacle course in your room. Explain that the teams will be competing in a relay race to complete the obstacle course. The catch is that each person must carry his or her team's Etch-a-Sketch while running the obstacle course. So after the first person on a team completes the course, he or she will hand the Etch-a-Sketch to the next person in line, who will then do the same thing, and so on. The first team to complete the course—without erasing the message on its Etch-a-Sketch—is the winner. If team members jostle the Etch-a-Sketch too much while running, they won't be able to read the message on the screen at the end of the game. Use this activity to lead in to a discussion of the things that prevent us from clearly receiving messages from God via prayer.

Step 5

As you wrap up the session, set up a "mini-prayer vigil" for your kids. Designate a day in the coming week for your vigil. Prepare a schedule divided into five-minute increments. Ask each of your kids to commit to praying for five minutes on your designated day by signing up for one of the sections on the schedule. Make sure that all of the slots on the schedule are filled so that you have a continuous prayer link going for at least a couple of hours. Hand out copies of a list of requests for your kids to pray about during the vigil. Have kids write down the time they signed up for on their list of requests. At your next meeting, discuss how the prayer vigil went.

Step 2

Kids may have heard prayer described as "two-way" communication, but find the idea confusing or frustrating—and ignore it as just another meaningless Christian cliché. How can prayer be "two-way" when God doesn't say anything? Take care not to imply that kids are supposed to hear God's side of the "conversation." Point out that God can communicate with a voice if He wants to, but He hasn't promised to. Instead, He may help us remember something we've read in His Word. Or He might guide our thoughts in a certain direction. Instead of emphasizing the two-way idea, you may want to observe simply that when we focus only on ourselves and our needs when we pray, we aren't giving God first place.

Step 4

If kids have heard of "journaling," they probably associate it with super-saints or English class assignments. Your chances of convincing most kids to "journal" are remote, but you may be able to help them relate to the process. Give each person an index card and a pencil. Say: **On one side of your card, do either of the following: (1) Pretend you've been keeping a diary of the ups and downs of your friendships. Jot down three items you might have included last week. (2) Pretend you've been keeping a maintenance record on your family car—tracking repairs, oil changes, accidents. Jot down three items you might have included in the last six months.** When kids have completed that assignment, ask them to turn their cards over and either (1) do the same with notes on their "friendship" with God during the last week, or (2) do the same with notes on how well they've "maintained" their relationship with God during the last six months.

Step 2

Hand out paper and pencils. Ask your group members to write down three questions about prayer. These may be general questions, personal inquiries, or things their friends may have asked. Collect the questions. Then have your group members try to answer each other's questions to the best of their ability. By working together as a group, with a little insight from you, kids may surprise themselves with how much they already know. And even if this isn't the case, they will at least find answers for their questions.

Step 3

The session deals with portions of the Sermon on the Mount before and after the Lord's Prayer (Matthew 6:9-13). Yet it may be that the Lord's Prayer is essentially all some of your kids know about praying. If so, use it as a natural starting point for them. Point out that memorizing the specific words isn't what Jesus was suggesting. Rather, the Lord's Prayer makes an excellent *outline* for our own prayers. It starts by focusing on who God is and submitting to His will. It moves on to personal daily needs. It concludes with an emphasis on God's forgiveness and a reminder that we live in an evil world. Encourage your group members not just to memorize the prayer as a "quickie" prayer for emergencies, but rather to use it as a starting point for expressing all of the things on their mind.

Step 1

Begin the session by playing some worship music, the lyrics of which describe the power, might, and strength of God. (An excellent tape with songs on this theme is *Praise and Worship, Mighty God* from Hosanna! Music.) Songs you may want to play include "Lift Up Your Voices," "My Help Comes from the Lord," and "Mighty Is Our God." After playing (and singing, if your kids know the words) these songs, ask: **When you think of the strength and power of God, how do you feel?** (Some may find comfort in these things; others may find fear.) If no one mentions it, ask if anyone ever feels intimidated by God, especially when they think of praying to Him. Allow time for responses.

Step 5

If your junior highers are somewhat mature, a great way to build fellowship among your group members is to set up prayer partner arrangements. There are a number of ways that you can do this. For instance, you might pair up kids (preferably ones who know each other well) to pray for the needs of their partner during the week. Or, rather than pairing individuals, you might set up "prayer teams" and instruct kids to pray for the members of their team during the week. Or you might set up a prayer chain. When a need arises, one person in the chain calls another to pass along a prayer need. That person will then call the next person in the chain, and so on. (However, you need to be careful to prevent the prayer chain from becoming a gossip chain.) Or you might let kids offer their ideas for a prayer partner arrangement. The options are endless.

Step 1

After you've discussed the answers to Repro Resource 3, refer back to the sheet. Say: **Now we're going to roleplay these situations to see what interrupting can lead to.** Ask for volunteers to roleplay each couple of lines, taking the conversation a few lines further. Encourage some of the pairs to keep interrupting each other. Encourage others to realize what they've done and apologize. Try to get a variety of responses. Afterward, discuss as a group the different reactions and how the people may have felt in each scenario.

Step 4

Ask: **What do you do when you have something you need to share, but have no one to share it with?** If no one mentions it, suggest writing in a diary. If you wish, read a few lines from *Anne Frank: The Diary of a Young Girl.* Say: **Keeping a diary is one way many people choose to "get out" thoughts and feelings that they have no one else to tell.** Ask if any of your girls keep a diary. Then explain that there's a way we can keep a diary of our prayers; it's called journaling. Keeping a journal is a lot like keeping a diary. Explain the ACTS model and continue Step 4 as written.

Step 2

If you have an athletic group of guys, many of them are probably familiar with the important role a coach can play in their lives. If so, eliminate Repro Resource 4 and spend time instead trying to help kids see that God acts as the best coach they could ever want. Ask: **In what ways is listening to God sort of like listening to a coach?** (We need to know the "playbook"—the Bible—which tells us what to do in many specific situations we will encounter. The coach sees things shaping up long before most of the players do. The coach speaks from experience that players don't have. A good coach not only wants to win, but also wants his players to be the best possible individuals they can be. A coach is a teacher, motivator, counselor, and friend.) Explain that prayer is how we keep in contact with our Coach. Bible reading is certainly important, but it's the personal communication of prayer that keeps us strong.

Step 4

Keeping a journal may sound like "writing in a diary" to some guys—something that's "for girls." If you think this might be true of your guys, prepare to confront this attitude by going to a library before the session and collecting several examples of literature from the journals of famous men. You can find writings of historical figures, well-known writers, church fathers, contemporary Christians, and much more. For example, Jim Eliot kept a journal before being killed by the Auca Indians. C. S. Lewis kept a journal as well. Many of the world's great men kept up their journals throughout their lifetimes. Show your guys that maintaining a journal doesn't guarantee fame, but it certainly doesn't hurt, either.

Step 1

Have kids form pairs and take them outside. Instruct the members of each pair to put as much distance between themselves as possible. Ideally, partners should be out of hearing range of each other. Give one person in each pair a message to try to communicate to the other. (Assign different messages to each pair.) With the partners extremely far apart, have each person try to communicate his or her message. No one should be able to do so at first, so move the listeners a little closer and have the speakers try again. Keep moving the listeners a few steps closer until someone is finally able to hear what is being said. (The listener must be able to repeat the message word for word.) Use this activity to demonstrate the fact that sometimes God may be wanting to communicate with us. But if we've wandered too far away, we miss what He's trying to say. Sometimes we recognize that He's there, but we're not close enough to hear clearly what He is saying. The purpose of prayer is to get close enough to God to communicate clearly with Him.

Step 4

If you don't think kids will keep up with individual journals, try a group journal. Starting this week, give kids an opportunity to jot down their feelings, thoughts, frustrations, desires, or whatever they wish. A "prayer journal" sounds a bit somber, so use the concept of a "group journal" even though you might want to keep up with prayer requests as well. If a few kids volunteer to write a few sentences each week, they may be surprised at how quickly they create a written history of the group. The journal will be an excellent resource to recall good memories, to find comfort during future hard times, and to see how God works on a regular basis.

Step 1

Show one or more "dysfunctional conversation" scenes from the following videos (after pre-screening them for appropriateness):

• *Wayne's World 2.* In an early scene, Wayne, Garth, and friends pull up to a fast-food drive-through and place an order, leaving out key words in an effort to drive the order-taker crazy—but the latter still gets it right. Ask: **What tends to get left out of your prayers? Do you think God understands our prayers even if we don't pray them "right"? Why or why not?**

• *Ghost.* Play a scene in which fake medium Whoopi Goldberg has a hard time communicating with the deceased Patrick Swayze, whom she can hear but not see. Ask: **Is this like prayer? How is it different? Why do you suppose God usually doesn't communicate with us in a voice that we can hear?**

• *Indiana Jones and the Last Crusade.* Show the scene in which Indy (Harrison Ford) is trying to have a rare, meaningful conversation with his father (Sean Connery), who acts as if there's no need to talk. Ask: **When you pray, do you find God to be this kind of "father"? Or is God more interested in having a good talk with you than you are in having one with Him? Why?**

Step 3

During the week before the session, record the touch-tone "beeps" made when you telephone the home of each group member. On paper, keep track of which sounds go with each person's phone. To start the step, play the tape of the tones. See whether kids can guess which sounds match their home phones. Award a prize for each correct guess. Then ask: **When it comes to prayer, do you think God knows your personal "number"? Is He interested in hearing from you, or just from humans in general? Why?**

Step 1

Stage a "Knees and Elbows Race" (preferably on a lawn or carpeted floor). Have kids line up side by side. Give each person four pieces of uncooked elbow macaroni. At your signal, each person must put one piece behind each of his or her knees and one in the crook of each of his or her elbows—and get to the finish line across the room or lawn. The first to reach the finish line with all four pieces wins. Kids will soon discover that they must walk on their knees and keep their arms bent to make this work. After awarding a prize, ask: **Did you have a good prayer time during this race?** (No.) **But you were on your knees. Isn't that what prayer is all about?** Discuss the difference between "going through the motions" of prayer and making prayer a way to grow closer to God.

Step 3

Replace Steps 3, 4, and 5 with the following activity. Have volunteers read aloud Psalm 102:1-17. Then discuss: **When have you felt most like the writer of this psalm? Have you ever prayed a prayer like this? Why or why not? What kind of relationship does the person seem to have with God? What do you think happened before the person asked God for help? What does the person want God to do? What does the person talk about, other than making requests?** If possible, play a contemporary Christian "psalm" that addresses God. Possibilities include "Sincerely Yours" (Gary Chapman), "Here I Am" (Russ Taff), "Do I Trust You" (Twila Paris), "A Way" (Michael W. Smith), and "Sparrow Watcher" (Pam Mark Hall). Close the session by having kids write brief psalm-prayers that (1) thank God for something He's done and (2) ask Him to do something in the future.

Step 3

Bring in an old record player and three non-valuable records. Remove the needle from the record player. Announce that you've got some songs you want your kids to hear. Explain that a friend of yours told you that the songs were excellent. Put the first record on the turntable. Say: **Now, listen closely.** Nothing should happen. Lift the record arm and place it down further on the record. When nothing happens, act frustrated. Say: **I can't believe this! My friend said this song was great. There must be something wrong with this record!** Angrily lift the record from the turntable and smash it. Repeat this process with the other two records, growing increasingly angry and claiming that you will never trust your friend again. Then calmly stop your act. Say: **What do you think? Was there really anything wrong with the records? Maybe the problem was with the record player itself. You know what? Sometimes we do the same thing to our relationship with God. We don't feel close to God so we "trash" the relationship. Maybe the problem is not with God. Maybe it's something in our life—something like a lack of prayer—that creates a barrier, just like the broken needle.**

Step 5

As a group, brainstorm some prayer requests that stem from living in an urban environment. Perhaps one of your kids is worried about gang infiltration in his or her neighborhood. Perhaps another person is concerned about not having a safe place to play after school. Whatever the requests, help your group members recognize that God is concerned with every one of their requests, no matter how minor or trivial it may seem. Close the session with a time of prayer in which you take your kids' requests before the Lord.

Step 4

After explaining the ACTS model of prayer, hand out paper and pencils. Give kids an opportunity to do some journaling, using ACTS as a model. Be sure to explain that no matter what method we use to pray, there's no "right" or "wrong" way to do it. Some people may feel very comfortable using ACTS as a guide. Some may wish to write poetry. Some may need to "dump out" their feelings to God. Whatever the method, assure your group members that their prayers are personal communication between them and God.

Step 5

Offer your group members—especially your high schoolers—an opportunity for some accountability in the changes they've said they need to make. It's very easy to say that we need to change something and even promise that we will. It's much more difficult, however, to stick to it and actually do it. Set up a partner program to allow your group members to share with each other what they've identified as needing to work on. Encourage them to be specific. Then, at your next meeting, allow time for your "accountability partners" to share with each other how their weeks went. Encourage them to continue their relationship as the year goes on.

Step 1

Instead of using Repro Resource 3, try another opening activity. Before the session, write the words to the children's prayer "Now I Lay Me Down to Sleep" on index cards, one word per card. Prepare three sets of cards. To begin the session, have kids form three teams. Give each team one set of cards, making sure that the cards in each set are well-scrambled. See which team can arrange its cards in the proper order first. Award prizes to the winning team. Afterward, ask: **How many of you have prayed this prayer before? What other kinds of things do you pray to God about? How often do you pray? What keeps you from praying more?**

Step 4

Rather than using the spelling bee activity with your sixth graders, simply ask: **Is there anything that you would rather write to someone in a note than say to them out loud? If so, what? Why is writing sometimes easier than talking?** Use group members' responses to lead in to a discussion of journaling.

Date Used: _____

Approx.
Time

Step 1: Let Me Finish! _____
o Extra Action
o Large Group
o Fellowship & Worship
o Mostly Girls
o Extra Fun
o Media
o Short Meeting Time
o Sixth Grade
Things needed:

Step 2: It's a Two-Way Street _____
o Heard It All Before
o Little Bible Background
o Mostly Guys
Things needed:

Step 3: Call-Waiting _____
o Extra Action
o Small Group
o Little Bible Background
o Media
o Short Meeting Time
o Urban
Things needed:

Step 4: Write It Down! _____
o Heard It All Before
o Mostly Girls
o Mostly Guys
o Extra Fun
o Combined Junior High/High School
o Sixth Grade
Things needed:

Step 5: Personalizing Your Prayer Closet _____
o Small Group
o Large Group
o Fellowship & Worship
o Urban
o Combined Junior High/High School
Things needed:

3 Why Praise God?

YOUR GOALS FOR THIS SESSION:

Choose one or more

☐ To help kids recognize that God is worthy of praise.

☐ To help kids understand why Christians are called to praise God.

☐ To help kids begin to praise God—both in corporate worship settings and in the way they live their lives.

☐ Other _____

Your Bible Base:

Psalms 149:1-6; 150
Matthew 18:20
Romans 12:1, 2
Revelation 3:15, 16

OPTIONS

STEP 1

Tell 'em How Great They Are

(Needed: Chairs)

Have kids arrange their chairs in a circle in order to play the "Compliment Game." Have someone stand in the middle of the circle. Explain that group members must, one at a time, compliment the person standing in the middle. Have those in the circle keep a fairly steady rhythm with their compliments (either by feet-stomping or hand-clapping). If a person doesn't pay a compliment in time or gives a previously-stated compliment, that person must bow down to the person in the middle and chant "I'm not worthy" three times. Then resume the compliments until everyone has given one. Continue until everyone has had a chance to stand in the middle of the circle.

Afterward, ask: **What are some different ways that people react to being praised or complimented? How did it feel for you to be praised and complimented?** Get several responses.

Then say: **Let's take a look at someone else who is often praised and complimented. The funny thing is that this Person doesn't need others' praise. And it probably does more good for those who do the praising than it does for Him.**

STEP 2

Brush with Greatness

(Needed: Small paintbrushes, watercolor paints, glasses of water, newsprint or butcher paper, prize)

Hand out paintbrushes (the small, skinny kind used in art classes). Have kids form pairs. Give each pair a large piece of newsprint or butcher paper, a set of watercolor paints, and a glass of water (for rinsing).

Explain that you want each person to paint one thing that he or she thinks is great about God. Emphasize that group members are free to paint anything they want, but that they should be prepared to explain how their picture describes God's greatness.

After kids have finished this assignment, instruct them to paint a picture that shows their favorite way to worship God. Point out that singing hymns in church isn't the only way to praise God. Things like playing an instrument, playing a sport, drawing, speaking, acting, and giving one's best effort in work and at school all can be forms of worship. When everyone is finished, have kids display and explain their masterpieces. Then let group members vote on their favorite portrait. Award a prize to the winning artist.

Afterward, say: **We've seen several different ways that people can worship God. It may be through singing—or it may not. God's probably glad that singing isn't the only form of worship, considering some of our voices. But it's not the method of worship He's concerned with, anyway. He desires to be worshiped by us because He knows that we'll be the ones who benefit. Let's find out how and why worship is important for us.**

STEP 3

Everything That Hath Breath

(Needed: Bibles, copies of Repro Resource 5, pencils, chalkboard and chalk or newsprint and marker, stopwatch, prizes)

Have kids pair up for a breath-holding contest. When you say, **Go** (and start a stopwatch), one person in each pair will hold his or her breath while his or her partner watches. When the person finally takes a breath, the partner must raise his or her hand. The last person whose partner hasn't raised his or her hand is the winner. Announce the person's time when he or she finally takes a breath. Then have partners switch roles. Award prizes to the winner of each round.

Then have kids turn to Psalm 150. Ask someone to read the psalm aloud, focusing specifically on verse 6. Afterward, say: **Obviously, since all of us seem to be breathing, we can't escape the Bible's call to worship God. Why do you think the psalmist placed such an emphasis on praising and worshiping God?** (Perhaps the psalmist knew how it would benefit those who praised God. Perhaps the psalmist felt it was the duty of God's people.)

Have someone read aloud Matthew 18:20. Then ask: **What are some different instances in which people get together in God's name?** Emphasize the importance of corporate worship in drawing closer to God.

Have someone reread Psalm 150. Then read Psalm 149:1-6. Discuss as a group some of the different instruments these psalms mention as being part of praising God.

Hand out copies of "Strike Up the Band" (Repro Resource 5). After a few minutes, ask volunteers to share what they came up with. Then ask: **Do you think you could use your band to worship God? Why or why not?** Help your group members see that God can be praised in any musical style.

If you're not musically inclined, and not likely to start a band in the near future, what are some other creative ways that you could praise God with a group of your friends? Encourage kids to be as creative as possible in their suggestions. Write kids' ideas on the board as they're named. (You'll refer to them later in the session.)

Actions Speak Louder Than Words

(Needed: Bibles, copies of Repro Resource 6, pencils)

Have someone read aloud Romans 12:1, 2. Then ask: **What do you think it means to offer our bodies as living sacrifices that are pleasing to God?** (Perhaps it means that we are to praise and worship God not merely through ritual activity, but also in the way we live, with all of our heart, mind, and will.)

What does being "transformed by the renewing of your mind" have to do with worship? (When we demonstrate by the way we live that we are different from the non-Christian world, in a sense, we are directing praise to God, the source of our transformation.)

As a group, brainstorm some specific examples of how the principles of Romans 12:1, 2 might be demonstrated by Christians. Examples might include things like keeping our minds and bodies sexually pure, keeping a check on any bad attitudes, watching our language and speech habits, and avoiding harmful substances like alcohol and drugs.

Ask: **How does it make you feel to know that you can wor-**

ship God in the way you live? Explain. Get responses from several group members.

Ask kids to call out the names of some things that are bad when they're lukewarm. Some examples might include hot chocolate, pizza, bath water, etc. Then have someone read aloud Revelation 3:15, 16. Ask: **How might this passage relate to our worship of God?** (God is not looking for half-hearted praise from us. He wants us to be "on fire" in our worship for Him. If we're not excited about worship, we shouldn't just go through the motions.)

Hand out copies of "What's That You Say?" (Repro Resource 6). Give group members a few minutes to complete the sheet. When everyone is finished, discuss as a group the importance of truly reflecting what's in our hearts when we worship God.

Refer back to the list of creative worship ideas you wrote on the board in Step 3. Encourage group members to choose one of the ideas on the board (or come up with one of their own) to put into practice in the coming week in order to "spark" their worship and praise of God.

Close the session with a group worship time. Let your kids request some of their favorite praise and worship choruses for the group to sing together. Take as many requests as time allows.

Strike Up the Band

One Friday afternoon after school, the phone rings. It's for you.

"Is this _____?" asks a voice on the other end of the line.

"Yes, it is," you answer, a bit hesitantly.

"Well, you've been randomly chosen as the winner of the Tricky Ricky Records grand-prize drawing! Do you have any idea what you've just won?"

After a few seconds, you remember that you signed up at a local music store to win a record deal with one of the music industry's major companies.

"I've won a record deal?!" you scream into the phone.

"That's right," says Tricky Ricky. "An all-expense paid record deal for you and your band. Last year's winner, the Talking Donkeys, cut an album that went platinum."

All of a sudden, Tricky Ricky's words hit you: "you *and your band*." You don't *have* a band. Never did. You just said you did because you had to have one to be eligible to win.

Your head is buzzing, so Tricky Ricky's final words don't really register with you as you hang up the phone. You do remember him saying something about having you and your band at the record company Monday morning, prepared to play a couple of songs.

Your mind races. Who, among your friends, will be in your band? What instruments will they play? Who will sing? What will be the band's name? What style of music will you play? What will be the titles of your first two songs?

Don't worry if you or your friends don't play instruments or sing well. You've got the whole weekend to become accomplished musicians and singers. But first, you've got to get everything set up. Get going!

Name of the band:

Style of music you'll play:

Lead singer:

Instruments in the band:

Who will play what in the band:

Names of your band's first two songs:

What's That You Say?

Do you ever wonder if sometimes, when mankind is singing and worshiping God, God ever asks, "What's that you say?" You know, when He hears one thing from us, but sees another? It's tough to always stay consistent both in our worship to God and in our daily living. But below are a few questions that may help. Answer them as honestly as possible. (Don't worry, your answers are just between you and God.)

The Bible states that we're all sinners (Romans 3:23), but it also states that if we confess our sins to God, He will forgive us for them (I John 1:9). Are there some sins in your life that you know you haven't confessed to God? If so, what are some of the areas in your life that are holding you back from truly worshiping God?

Describe a time in your life when you felt close to God, when you know you truly worshiped Him.

Step 2

Instead of using the painting activity, take the group to your church sanctuary (assuming that it's empty). Say: **Show me the best place to sit if you want to goof off during the service.** Let kids sit to show their opinions; ask a few to explain. Then say: **Show me the best place to sit if you want to pay close attention to the sermon.** Kids should rearrange themselves and explain. Say: **Now show me where to sit if you want to get the best sound from the music.** Kids should move and explain. Say: **Now show me where to sit if you want to feel close to God.** Let kids move and explain. Then say: **Now show me where to sit if you really want to worship God.** Let kids move and explain. Ask: **If the audience sits in the pews and the participants are on the platform, where should you sit if you want to worship God?** (On the platform, since God is the audience.) Sitting as a group on the platform, discuss the mistaken idea that during worship we are the audience and the "platform people" are the participants. Note that we can worship from any spot as long as we remember that we're the players, not the spectators.

Step 4

Point out that some people say they don't need to go to church to worship; they can do that anywhere. Have kids form teams, assigning an adult helper to each team. Have each team walk to a different spot in your neighborhood (a park, a street corner, a church member's garage, etc.) and attempt to (a) sing a praise chorus, and (b) pray sentence prayers of praise. After a certain amount of time, regather the group and discuss what happened. Were some places better for worship than others? If singing and praying didn't work, what might have been better? What kinds of worship might work best at school? At home? At church?

Step 1

In a small group, you can try a written variation of the "Compliment Game." This will give kids something to take home and keep for times when they need it. Give everyone a small paper bag, a pencil, and several sheets of paper. Kids should write their names on the bags, which should then be placed at a central location in the room. Group members should then write out compliments for each other. (Make it extremely clear that nothing but positive comments may be written on these sheets!) Everyone in the room should write something (or several things) to every other person. The writers need not identify themselves. When they finish, group members should deliver their compliment sheets to the respective paper bags. Give kids a few minutes to read what's been written about them. Then discuss how it feels to be praised and complimented.

Step 2

Explain that another way to "compliment" each other is to work together. For example, one person's outgoing personality "complements" another's shyness. Within a small group, it is important for people to learn to "complement" each other as well as to "compliment" each other. With this in mind, have your group members work *together* on a poster of praise to God. One person might come up with a good theme; another might have an idea for a general design. One person might use artistic talent to draw everything in place; others might fill in the colors and add specifics. Make sure that everyone contributes something unique to the poster. Afterward, explain that God is less honored by a piece of cardboard and a little color than by the fact that part of His "body" worked together to accomplish something for Him.

Step 1

Before the session, write the words to a well-known hymn or praise song on index cards, one word or phrase per card. As kids arrive, give each of them a card. Explain that group members must arrange themselves in the correct order, according to the lyrics of the song. When kids have what they think is the correct order, ask them to sing the song, with each person singing his or her word or phrase. (If kids don't know the tune, they should make one up.) Afterward, play a tape of the song so that kids can hear how it really goes. Use this activity to introduce the idea of singing praises to God.

Step 4

Hand out copies of your church's bulletin. As a group, go over the components of your church's worship service one item at a time, deciding how each aspect lends (or doesn't lend) itself to worship. Then have kids form three groups. Instruct the members of each group to design their own worship service, incorporating components of your church's worship as well as other items that they come up with. To make the activity a little more challenging, you might have one group plan a service for younger children, one group plan a service for teens, and one group plan a service for residents of a nursing home. After a few minutes, have each group share its plan. Note the similarities and differences between worship plans.

Step 2

Kids may automatically paint pictures of mountains or sunsets without really thinking about the greatness of God. They may also paint "favorite" worship methods without really liking *any* kind of worship. Or they may paint whatever worship method is easiest to depict. So instead of using the painting activity, have kids form teams. Give each team a different kind of magazine (computers, sports, travel, entertainment, music, etc.). Instruct each team to tear pictures from its magazine, trying to find five that could somehow illustrate the greatness of God. To do this, teams will have to talk about why God is great; they'll also have to get creative as they explain their choices to the rest of the group. Instead of having kids paint pictures of favorite worship methods, ask whether kids *have* any favorites and why.

Step 3

If your kids are likely to yawn over Psalm 150, try instead passages in which people worshiped God in unusual situations. For example, in II Samuel 6:14-16, 20-23, David dances in a "praise parade." In Acts 16:22-31, Paul and Silas sing hymns in jail. In Job 1:13-22, Job praises God despite great loss. Ask: **Why do you think these people went to such lengths to praise God? What things, big and little, tend to keep you from praising God?**

Step 2

As soon as you begin to discuss the importance of praising God, ask your group members to work together to create a "top-ten list" of reasons to praise God. See what they come up with out of their limited knowledge of Scripture. It is somewhat unusual for people in our culture to praise someone else unless there are ulterior motives. See if this attitude is reflected in your group members' reasons to praise God. If it is, you can deal with it during the Bible study that follows. If not, you will still be better equipped to know where your kids stand spiritually as you present the rest of the session.

Step 4

Romans 12:1, 2 is not an easy passage for beginners. The Psalms references in the previous step are fairly self-explanatory, so be sure to save some time to discuss what it means to be a "living sacrifice" and to "renew one's mind." You will probably need to be prepared to do a quick review of the Old Testament system of sacrifices, of Jesus' sacrifice, and of related verses to make this passage relevant. Another option is to assign related passages and have kids read them during the following week. If your group members are new to the Bible, the best way to help them "catch up" is to challenge them to do so on their own. An hour a week in a group setting is a start, but kids need encouragement to establish a daily (or *almost* daily) Bible-reading regimen.

Step 1

After kids have finished playing the "Compliment Game" with each other, explain that now you're going to put in the middle the One who deserves all of the compliments and praise that we can offer—God. Place a Bible in the middle of the circle to represent God. Then have kids play the "Compliment Game" in the same manner as before, offering praise to God. Afterward, ask: **How did it feel to say or to hear someone else saying "I'm not worthy" at the "feet" of God?** Explain briefly that none of us is worthy of God's love; however, because He offers His love so freely, our natural response and desire should be to praise Him.

Step 4

Read Psalm 150 again; then do just what the psalm says. Praise God in His sanctuary. Praise Him in His mighty heavens by moving outside. Praise Him with the trumpet, with dancing, and with resounding cymbals. If you can't find a harp or lyre, you may need to improvise. Also, depending on the restrictions or limitations of your particular church, you may need to get creative. But remember, our God is a creative God, and He loves to hear His children's praise.

MOSTLY GIRLS

Step 2

If some of your girls have trouble coming up with their favorite way to worship God, ask them why. Some may say that worship is boring. Others may say that they can't relate to worship activities. As group members mention their reasons, make a list of them on the board. Then brainstorm as a group some ways for a person to enjoy worship more. Read Psalm 150. Then ask: **Does this sound like God wants us to be bored with worship?** (Obviously not!) **Looking at Psalm 150, what are some things you think we could do to liven up our worship?** If time permits, you may want to put some of your group members' suggestions into practice.

Step 4

Hand out paper and drawing materials (colored pencils, markers, crayons, or whatever else you prefer). Instruct your group members to draw what they think of when they hear the word "hypocrite." After a few minutes, have your girls display and explain their drawings. Then read aloud the following definition from *Webster's Dictionary:* "one who affects virtues or qualities he does not have." Ask: **Do any of you know Christians who are hypocrites?** Do *not* let anyone name names here. **How could a Christian be a hypocrite?** (By not living out the beliefs she professes to hold.) Field any questions this discussion may foster; then have someone read Romans 12: 1, 2 and continue Step 4 as written.

MOSTLY GUYS

Step 1

Complimenting other guys may feel a little strange for some of your group members. So rather than playing the "Compliment Game" as written, "trick" your guys into complimenting each other. Ask: **Who are some of the men that you most admire?** Write down kids' responses on the board. Then ask: **In what ways is** [the name of one of your group members] **like** [the first name on the list]**?** It may take a while for the comparisons to come, but they will. For example, while your first guy might not have the muscles of his most-admired linebacker, perhaps others will observe that "He always puts 100 percent effort into whatever he's doing." Eventually guys should see that their adult heroes were once kids too—like your group members are now. What matters most at *this* point is effort and hope—and both of these things are made easier with a little praise and a few compliments from others.

Step 4

Who says guys can't sing? Before the session, assemble a variety of praise music by all-male groups. Try to include a song by the Vienna Boys' Choir, an all-male gospel quartet number, a Gregorian chant, a bluegrass version of a hymn, a favorite male contemporary Christian group, and anything else that would show your guys that not all singing men sound alike. Then, as you sing some songs to conclude the session, explain to your guys that if they can't sing on key, they should at least sing loud. God appreciates the enthusiasm much more than He does the technical quality of the music.

EXTRA FUN

Step 1

Begin the session by playing dodge ball, with one person in the center being pelted by those around him or her. If dodge ball is not feasible, try a similar kind of game that inflicts a low level of pain on someone who isn't quick enough or alert enough. Play for a while, goading group members into being competitive and aggressive. Then suddenly shift from that game to the "Compliment Game." Afterward, ask: **Was it easier for you to get smacked with a ball or to receive genuine praise from your peers?** Some people are likely to prefer the former to the latter. Discuss their reasons.

Step 4

After group members complete Repro Resource 5, say: **Suppose we *as a group* were offered a recording contract. What should we do?** Go through the same issues that kids went through for Repro Resource 5—name of the band, music style, instrumentation, and so forth. But this time, kids must work *together* and agree on what to do. Afterward, you might actually do whatever kids suggest to the extent that you are able. The singers can sing. The musicians can play air guitar, air tuba, or whatever. The group roadies can set up the stage. Prepare at least two songs with your impromptu band. If you're successful, plan a road tour.

Step 2

Have kids form teams. Let the group watch TV or listen to the radio for at least three minutes. Have each team listen for "praise phrases" ("car of the year," "beautiful," "Baby, it's you," "world's largest," "supergroup," etc.) and write them down. The team that collects the most words and phrases wins. Afterward, ask: **Which of these phrases would apply to God? Why? Which aren't strong enough? What "praise phrases" would you add to describe God?**

Step 3

Compare and contrast the styles of worship found in scenes from the following videos (after pre-screening the scenes yourself).
• *Say Amen, Somebody.* Play one or more scenes from this spirited documentary in which African-American pioneers of Gospel music sing individually, in groups, and in choirs.
• *Agnes of God.* Show a scene in which the nuns pray, sing, or otherwise worship.
• *Tender Mercies.* Play the scene in which Mac (Robert Duvall) is baptized in a small, rural church.
   Ask: **Why do people worship God in different ways? How do you think He wants you to worship Him? Why?**

Step 1

Replace Steps 1 and 2 with a shorter opener. Before the session, ask one of your church's better bakers to come up with homemade refreshments for the meeting. As you serve the refreshments, bring in the baker and announce that she or he provided the food. Ask your group: **Is there anything you'd like to say to this person?** See what kids come up with. Then ask: **Other than just saying "Thank you," can you think of ways in which we could show our appreciation?** Have kids form teams. Give each team a hypothetical amount of money (ranging from a nickel to $500) to spend on showing appreciation. After a couple of minutes, have each group share its ideas. Use this activity to introduce the concept of praising God in a variety of ways.

Step 3

Skip Repro Resource 5. Also skip Step 4. Instead, read John 4:23, 24. Then ask: **What does it mean to worship in spirit?** (To worship with your heart, and not just go through the motions.) **What does it mean to worship in truth?** (To have the true God and His Son at the center of your worship.) If your church bulletins include an order of service, give each person a recent copy. After each item in the order of service, kids should draw one to five hearts (five being strongest) to show how involved their hearts usually are at each point in the worship. Kids should also draw one to five crosses after each item to show how well they tend to focus on God or Jesus at each point. (If your bulletins don't include an order of service, jot one down yourself and read it aloud as kids reply by drawing crosses and hearts on index cards.) Close with silent prayer in which kids can talk to God about how they've been worshiping Him.

Step 1

If you think your kids would be uncomfortable complimenting each other, try a variation of the "Compliment Game." Have kids arrange their chairs in a circle. Ask them to imagine that Michael Jordan or some other sports or entertainment celebrity is standing in the middle of the circle. Explain that each person will have five seconds to think of a comliment to give to the celebrity. If a person can't think of one in five seconds (or if he or she gives a compliment that's already been used), he or she is out. Continue until only one person remains. Afterward, ask: **What if it had been God in the middle of the circle? How might your compliments have been different? Why?** After you've received several responses, move on to Step 2.

Step 4

During your group worship time at the end of the session, give your kids an opportunity to praise God for things associated with living in an urban environment. Kids often hear about the pitfalls and drawbacks of living in an urban setting. But there are some advantages to city life. Ask your kids to consider some of these advantages as they praise God. Make the point that every day we have hundreds of things to praise God for—things that we often take for granted.

Step 1

For an added twist to the "Compliment Game," divide kids into two groups—a junior high group and a high school group. To begin the game, have your high schoolers sit in a circle; then have your junior highers enter one by one for their shower of compliments. After all of your junior highers have had a turn in the middle of the circle, switch the game around. Have your junior highers sit in a circle; then have your high schoolers enter the circle one by one for their compliments. Afterward, ask your junior highers: **How did it feel to be complimenting someone older and probably wiser than you?** See if any of them felt intimidated. Then ask your high schoolers: **How did it feel to receive so many compliments? Did it matter that the people offering them were younger than you?** Explain that some people may feel intimidated when they think of praising God, or may think that because He is all-powerful and all-knowing, He doesn't need or want our praise. The truth is that He wants us to praise and worship Him because He knows the benefits that we receive when we do.

Step 3

Instead of using Repro Resource 5 after reading Psalm 150, divide your group into teams of four or five, making sure to combine junior highers and high schoolers on each team. Have kids refer back to Psalm 150. Explain that each team will create an act of worship based on one of the commands from the psalm. Teams may wish to move outside to worship. They may wish to create a dance of worship. Whatever strikes their fancy, they may choose. Allow the teams time to pull together their act of worship. After several minutes, have each team present its act of worship for all to enjoy (and join in, if possible).

Step 1

If you think it might be difficult for your sixth graders to offer sincere compliments to each other, try another option. Have kids form pairs. Give the members of each pair five minutes to list as many different compliments as they can think of. When time is up, have each pair read its list. If a compliment was listed by more than one pair, each pair that listed the compliment must mark it out. The pair with the most remaining compliments on its list is the winner. Afterward, discuss as a group which compliments on the pairs' lists could apply to God. Lead in to Step 2.

Step 4

Rather than asking your kids to name things that are bad when they're lukewarm, demonstrate your point using refreshments. Serve some "hot" chocolate made from barely warm tap water. If possible, you might also want to serve mildly warm pizza. When kids react to the lukewarm refreshments, lead in to a discussion of Revelation 3:15, 16.

Date Used:

Approx. Time

Step 1: Tell 'em How Great They Are   _____
o Small Group
o Large Group
o Fellowship & Worship
o Mostly Guys
o Extra Fun
o Short Meeting Time
o Urban
o Combined Junior High/High School
o Sixth Grade
Things needed:

Step 2: Brush with Greatness   _____
o Extra Action
o Small Group
o Heard It All Before
o Little Bible Background
o Mostly Girls
o Media
Things needed:

Step 3: Everything That Hath Breath   _____
o Heard It All Before
o Media
o Short Meeting Time
o Combined Junior High/High School
Things needed:

Step 4: Actions Speak Louder Than Words   _____
o Extra Action
o Large Group
o Little Bible Background
o Fellowship & Worship
o Mostly Girls
o Mostly Guys
o Extra Fun
o Urban
o Sixth Grade
Things needed:

Why Fellowship?

YOUR GOALS FOR THIS SESSION:

Choose one or more

☐ To help kids recognize that spending time with other Christians doesn't necessarily have to be a boring or trying experience.

☐ To help kids understand why spending time with other Christians is important in building our Christian lives.

☐ To help kids establish fellowship opportunities in which they can both draw strength from and strengthen other Christians.

☐ Other _____

Your Bible Base:

Proverbs 27:17
Matthew 18:19, 20
II Corinthians 6:14-18

Staying Alive Outside the Hive

(Needed: Prizes)

Instruct group members to stand against the wall at one end of your meeting area. Explain that you're going to play a game called "The Swarm." Select one person to be "queen (or king) bee" of the swarm. The queen (or king) bee must stand in the middle of the room. When you yell, **Swarm,** the rest of the kids must try to get to the wall on the other side of the room without being "stung" (or tagged) by the queen (or king) bee. Those who get stung become "worker bees" and must link arms with the queen (or king) bee. Then, for the next round, the queen (or king) bee and all of the worker bees will try to tag (while remaining linked together) the rest of the group members who are trying to get back across the room. Obviously, the more rounds you play, the larger the "swarm" in the middle will become. Award prizes to the last few remaining kids who haven't been stung.

Afterward, ask the last few remaining "unstung" people: **How did it feel as the "swarm" was bearing down on you?** Get a few responses.

Then ask the entire group: **Has there ever been a time in your life when you felt like you were one of the only Christians around—and that other people were bearing down on you? If so, explain.**

Discuss as a group some reasons why people sometimes feel alone and under pressure as a Christian. For instance, it may seem to some kids that there are no other Christians at their school or workplace. Encourage your kids to discuss some of the struggles they go through when they're feeling alone.

Swimming Upstream in a Downstream World

(Needed: Copies of Repro Resource 7, pencils)

Hand out copies of "In the Minority at Majority Junior High" (Repro Resource 7) and pencils. Instruct kids to put an "X" next to the places in their school where, as Christians, they feel like they're in the minority. For example, one of your guys might put an "X" by the picture of the locker room because many guys talk crudely and tell dirty jokes there. One of your girls might put an "X" next to the picture of the lunchroom, where she often eats with a group of girls who gossip and spread false rumors about other girls that they don't like.

When all of your kids are finished, go over the sheet as a group. Then explain: **Most Christians probably feel like they're in the minority at some point in their lives. But to help us avoid that "me against the world" feeling, God has given Christians a solution—other Christians. Let's check out what the Bible has to say about the benefits of fellowshipping with other believers.**

Swords, Pyramids, and Lawnmower Blades

(Needed: Bibles)

To make the Bible study a little more interesting, use a "sword drill" approach. The first passage you should call out is Matthew 18:19, 20. When the first person to find the passage has finished reading it, ask: **What promise can a Christian take from this passage?** (If two

OPTIONS

LARGE GROUP

HEARD IT ALL BEFORE

LITTLE BIBLE BACKGROUND

SHORT MEETING TIME

or more Christians get together, God will be there with them.)

How does it make you feel to know that God is with you when you are with other Christians? Allow time for some discussion.

Call out the next passage: II Corinthians 6:14-18. When the first person to find the passage has finished reading it, ask: **Do you think this passage is telling Christians to have nothing to do with non-Christians? Why or why not?** Let kids offer their comments.

Suggest that this passage prohibits a cooperation and alignment of thoughts, beliefs, and lifestyles with non-believers. Point out that Jesus didn't treat sinners like the plague—just their sins. In fact, Jesus hung out with the sinners, sometimes even more so then he did with "religious" people.

Ask: **Based on the example of Jesus, who "partied" with non-Christians by attending feasts and social events, what are your feelings about partying with non-Christians in a non-Christian atmosphere?** Let kids discuss their views on this, but don't try to resolve the issue. Instead, simply point out that Jesus did indeed spend time *with* non-Christians, but was never sucked in by them. Also emphasize that Jesus had His "get away" times with fellow believers during which He was strengthened by the support of others.

Have kids form two teams for a "Human Pyramid Challenge." Explain that the team that can build the most levels of human bodies kneeling on top of one another in three minutes will be declared the winner. Emphasize that each level must be held for at least ten seconds to be counted.

After a winning team has been declared, explain that the more support (the number of people on the bottom level) a team's pyramid had, the more potential it had to build more levels. Relate this to the fact that Christians gain both strength and support from other Christians through fellowship, which then can enable them to build up God's kingdom.

Have your kids grab their Bibles one last time as you call out your last passage: Proverbs 27:17. When the first person to find the passage has finished reading it, ask: **How many of you have ever had to mow a lawn?** After a show of hands, point out that the first part of verse 17, "As iron sharpens iron," indicates that sharpening a piece of iron requires another piece of iron; in this process, both pieces are sharpened.

Ask: **What do you think happens to lawnmower blades as they cut more and more grass?** (The blades get duller and duller, and eventually have to be resharpened by a hard, metallic sharpening wheel.)

Suggest that if a Christian (i.e., a lawnmower) is out in the world ministering to those in need of God (i.e., cutting grass), eventually his or her blades will become dull and will need to be sharpened.

Summarize: **A Christian can get burned out if he or she**

never gets "resharpened" or revitalized. That's why Christians go to church, attend retreats, and fellowship together. It's this fellowship time that can get Christians back to their "cutting edge."

The Fun Factor

(Needed: Copies of Repro Resource 8, pencils, slips of paper with group members' names on them)

The idea of spending time with other Christians in order to sharpen each other's Christian walk may sound good to your kids—in theory. Putting it into practice could be another story.

Ask: **In your opinion, how does the fun that Christians have compare with the fun that non-Christians have? Explain.**

Distribute copies of "A Knee-Slapping, Rip-Roaring Good Time" (Repro Resource 8). Give kids a few minutes to work on the sheet. When they're finished, have them hand in their sheets to you. Read the examples that your kids came up with and vote on the best one.

Acknowledge that the examples on Repro Resource 8 are somewhat exaggerated, and that the real issue isn't whether or not every Christian is the life of the party. Instead, the issue is that Christians share a common bond—their relationship with Jesus—that transcends social makeup.

As a group, brainstorm some ways in which your kids can support each other. If you can't come up with a better idea, you might write group members' names on slips of paper and then have kids draw slips to determine "accountability partners" (making sure you pair up kids who attend the same school). Instruct each person to stick a Post-it™ note with a question mark on it on his or her partner's locker every morning, letting that person know that someone cares about how his or her day at school will go. By the end of the day, each person should stick another Post-it™ note on his or her partner's locker, with either a "happy face" or a "frown face" on it to indicate whether he or she had a good day or a rough day. This can help both partners know how to pray for each other better. Also encourage the partners to share their feelings frequently by talking with each other.

Strength in Numbers

(Needed: Refreshments)

Close the session with a time of group affirmation. This may involve singing some of your kids' favorite songs, as well as a time of sharing and prayer. And of course, you'll want to have some refreshments ready in order to send your kids away in good spirits!

Also try to plan a weekend group activity. An idea that might prove to be fun and interesting would be to have a Saturday night "camp out" outside the church. Then everyone could attend the Sunday morning worship service together. This activity would be a great opportunity for Christian fellowship.

In the
Minority at Majority
Junior High

Below are some illustrations of various areas located throughout your school. If your school is like most schools, there are probably areas where as a Christian, you sometimes feel in the minority. Place an "X" next to any of the places listed below where you feel this way. Feel free to add your own areas at the bottom if there are any we've left out. Be prepared to explain why you feel in the minority in each area.

A Knee-Slapping,
RIP-ROARING GOOD TIME

Some people believe that Christians don't know how to have a good time. They have some rather strange ideas about what Christians do for fun. Below are some slightly exaggerated examples of some people's ideas of "Christian fun." After reading these examples, come up with a far-fetched idea of your own.

Devin Doolittle
Devin doesn't get out much. He slithers to the family sofa on Friday nights and sometimes doesn't reappear until Sunday morning for church. When no one's around, his favorite thing to do is leave the TV on for several minutes while he turns off all of the other lights in the house. Then, in a moment of unbridled craziness, he turns the TV off and gleefully watches the glow from the TV screen slowly fade into darkness. Sometimes the experience lasts nearly thirty seconds.

Penny Rollzalot
Every Friday after school, as the other kids head off to friends' houses, Penny heads to the bank. There, she cashes in her weekly allowance—a $10 bill—for twenty rolls of pennies. When she gets home, she dumps all 1,000 pennies out of their rolls, starts her stopwatch, and rerolls the pennies as fast as she can. Doing this several times a night, Penny can now boast of rolling 1,000 pennies in under six minutes, as well as making the loudest noise in the offering plate on Sunday morning.

Joe Skripcher
On Saturday nights, Joe likes to randomly open his Bible to a page and guess how many words are on that page. After writing down his guess, he counts the actual number of words on the page. The number of words that his guess is off by is how many minutes he will brush his teeth that night. He's been doing this for a few years now, so he's gotten fairly accurate, usually guessing within ten words. You can imagine how his pearly whites must have glistened the time he forgot to include the footnotes at the bottom of the page in his total and was off by 237 words.

Now you make up a person and his or her idea of a rip-roaring good time.

Step 2

Rather than using Repro Resource 7, try another option. Have kids form pairs. Give each pair four small adhesive bandages and a ballpoint pen. At your signal, each pair must do the following *with each person using only one finger.* (1) Unwrap the bandages. (2) Decide in which four areas at school Christian kids are most likely to feel outnumbered, and write the names of those areas on the bandages. (3) Apply the bandages, two per partner. The first pair to accomplish all of this wins. Afterward, discuss as a group the school areas that kids chose and the fact that it was easier to get the needed "first aid" when a partner helped.

Step 4

Skip Repro Resource 8. Instead, have kids wander around the room. Each person should call out repeatedly the name of his or her favorite TV show. Kids calling out the same show should group together. After half a minute, see how many groups have been formed and how many kids are partnerless. Have kids break up again and mill around. Each person should call out the name of his or her favorite recording artist or band, with groups forming on that basis. After half a minute, see what's happened. Then try it one more time, with kids calling out the initials of their favorite Savior (J.C., one would hope)—and grouping accordingly. After half a minute, all or most kids should be in the same group. (If some aren't, note mentally who they are, but don't make them feel conspicuous.) Use this activity as an illustration of the fact that we may not have much in common—except for our involvement in the group and, ideally, our faith in Christ.

Step 1

The "Swarm" game won't work well if you have only three or four kids. Instead, conduct an individual competition. Set up a table at one end of the room that will provide a decent-sized working area for each person. At the other end of the room, dump a large pile of some kind of building materials (wooden blocks, Legos, dominoes, or whatever). Explain that the object of the game is to see who can assemble the tallest structure out of the building materials in three minutes. The structures must be assembled on the table, and individuals may carry only one piece at a time. Give a signal and start the timer. At the end of three minutes, give another signal to stop. Measure to see whose structure is tallest and announce the winner. But then have kids take a look at how much they assembled one piece at a time. Say: **If you'd been working together, just think what you could have assembled!** Use this activity as a starting point to get kids thinking about what might be accomplished in their group, one person at a time. Also refer back to this activity in Step 3 instead of using the human pyramid activity.

Step 4

Rather than drawing names for "accountability partners," have kids commit to *all* of the other people in the group. Offer the locker-notes idea as one suggestion, but then challenge your kids to come up with something they *all* can do to encourage each other on a regular basis throughout the week. Suggestions might include eating lunch together, forming a telephone chain to pass along positive comments, and agreeing to wear the same piece of clothing or jewelry on a certain day to remind kids of each other. Kids may surprise you (and each other) with some of the good ideas they come up with.

Step 3

Before you start the sword drill, have kids compete in a four-legged race. Divide the group into teams of three. Tie two members of each team together as you would for a three-legged race. Then tie the third person to one of the two in the same manner. You should have one person in the middle who has both legs tied to another person. Have the teams race to see which can get to the other end of the room and back in the shortest amount of time. Award prizes to the winning team. The four-legged race activity should lead naturally into the first passage of your sword drill—Matthew 18:19, 20 ("where two or three come together in my name, there I am with them").

Step 4

Rather than handing out Repro Resource 8, read aloud one or two of the examples on the sheet. Then have kids form groups. Instruct each group to come up with a brief skit that shows another exaggerated example of a Christian having a "fun" time. Encourage kids to be humorous and creative in their skits, but not to be offensive or hurtful. After a few minutes, have each group perform its skit. Afterward, continue the session as written, beginning with the fourth paragraph in Step 4.

Step 1

Kids may have heard one too many times that non-Christian peers are "bearing down on" them—as if schools were filled with roving bands of pagans out to corrupt Christians by force. Kids know it's more common for young people to be attracted to "cool" kids and adopt their values in order to be "cool" themselves. To maintain credibility as you discuss peer pressure, avoid assuming that kids feel "swarmed" or "in the minority." First, ask *them* to describe how they feel about being around non-Christians at school. If some of your kids attend Christian schools, get their perspectives, too. If group members don't seem as concerned about peer pressure as the session assumes, address the subject as preparation for the bigger, possibly more hostile, world kids will face as they go to high school, college, and into the work force.

Step 3

Kids may question the assertion that going to church "sharpens" them. They may see Christian activities as "dulling"—or at least dull. Either skip the Proverbs 27:17 discussion and concentrate on mutual support or be prepared to give concrete examples of how being part of a youth group keeps Christians "sharp." If you choose the second option, share how leading the group keeps you on your toes spiritually. Ask kids who've participated in mission trips, summer camps, or service projects to explain how they were challenged by those activities.

Step 2

If your kids don't know the Bible because they've just recently gotten involved with your church or youth group, they may be in an excellent position to respect both Christians and non-Christians. When you get to Repro Resource 7, change the instructions a bit. Rather than having kids mark places where they feel "in the minority," have them try to break down all of the locations into "Christians" and "non-Christians." Then discuss what *they* should do in each location. When Christians are around, they can look for encouragement and strength. When non-Christians are around, they need to be aware of setting a positive Christian example and perhaps look for opportunities to invite those friends to the youth group. If group members learn to be more active wherever they are, they are less likely to ever feel in a minority.

Step 3

The fact that Jesus "partied" with non-Christians is used as a passing comment in the session. But this may be a side of the Son of God that people new to the Bible and your group are unaware of. Just as one example, have group members look up and read Matthew 9:9-13. While they may be amazed that Jesus spent a lot of time hanging out with sinful people, be sure they also realize *why* He did so. Ask: **What did Jesus mean by "It is not the healthy who need a doctor, but the sick"? In what ways can *we* begin to serve as "doctors" to those around us?**

Step 1

Provide paper and collage materials for your group members. Ask each person to create a picture of the image that comes to mind when he or she hears the word "fellowship." Encourage kids to be honest. After a few minutes, invite volunteers to share and explain what they came up with. You may find that your kids think of fellowship as an obligatory and boring part of being a Christian. Next, ask group members to think of their best friend and make a list of reasons why that person is their best friend. After a minute or so, invite volunteers to share their reasons. You'll probably find a common thread of "We like to do the same things" or "We have common interests." Say: **If our best friends are people with whom we share interests, and the definition of fellowship is "community of interest, activity, feeling, or experience," why do we say we don't enjoy fellowship with other Christians? Don't we have a lot in common with fellow Christians?**

Step 5

For your worship time, include songs that are based on the theme of unity and sharing our walk with others. You may also wish to read Matthew 18: 19, 20 again. Close the session by thanking God for His promise to be with us, especially when we're in fellowship with other believers.

Step 1

No other word sends chills of fear down the spine of a junior high girl quite like the word "cliques." Some of your girls may belong to a clique; all of your girls are affected by cliques. Ask: **What comes to mind when you hear the word "clique"?** Answers will vary, depending on whether or not your girls are part of a clique. **Why do you think cliques exist?** (For friendship, unity, and identity.) **What does it take to be part of a clique?** Get several responses. Then ask: **When you're not part of a clique— or halfheartedly part of one that doesn't really fit your style or beliefs—how do you feel? Why?** Lead in to a discussion of feeling alone as a Christian.

Step 4

After your girls have completed Repro Resource 8, say: **It probably wasn't too difficult to come up with something that a boring Christian would do. Now let's come up with a real good time for a real Christian.** Kids often link "don't" or "can't" with Christianity, so it may be a challenge for them to come up with ideas. Encourage them to be as creative and crazy as they can be.
After a few minutes, have volunteers share some of their ideas. Then say: **God didn't create us to be bored or boring. He's a** *creative* **God who wants** *us* **to be creative, enjoy life, and have fun.**

Step 2

Sometimes guys don't mind being in the minority. If they have confidence in themselves during sports or mental contests, being outnumbered is just another challenge that makes life interesting. So after your group members fill out Repro Resource 7, say: **Suppose we're strategizing how to "take over" the school, but we're in the minority as Christians. What should be our strategy?** Let guys theorize. For example, if the Christian/non-Christian ratio is about 50/50 in English class, they might want to start there. With a little effort, a majority could be achieved. Then they might want to turn their attention to certain areas of the lunchroom, and so forth. Eventually, they might even get around to the locker room. Challenge each guy this week to do at least one thing that will be a positive Christian influence to help counteract something sinful that other people may be doing.

Step 5

Help your group members plan a special out-of-the-ordinary "guy thing." Let them determine whether it should be a time they will use to get to know each other better, or if they would rather use the opportunity to invite their non-Christian friends to prove that Christians *do* know how to have fun. Challenge them to think big, but you should be aware of the available budget so that they don't plan something they can't actually carry out.

Step 2

Instead of using Repro Resource 7 as written, let kids *act out* their opinions. Have a volunteer roleplay a roving reporter, narrating his or her walk through the school. The other kids should act like typical students in each of the locations. For example, the reporter might begin by saying, "Here we are, entering Majority Junior High just before classes are about to begin. Let's see what these two girls are talking about." (The "reporter" should then hold the microphone toward two volunteers who will create a typical conversation.) As the reporter roams from room to room, other volunteers should roleplay various students and offer input in character.

Step 5

As you're sitting around having refreshments, ask your kids to imagine that they are professional church consultants who have just attended an average meeting of your youth group. It is their job to give you some input. Ask your "consultants": **How can this group have more fun on a regular basis? Any group can go out and do stuff, but what would it take for us to have more fun week by week during our meetings?** Let kids respond as "professionals." Keep things lighthearted and fun, but take what they say seriously. Perhaps there are a number of things you can adapt, eliminate, shorten, revise, or "tweak" in some way that would make kids more comfortable. And if they are truly wise consultants, they'll realize that the responsibility of having fun is only slightly up to the leader. Enthusiasm must generate from the group members, or the overall fun level will suffer. (If your consultants come to this conclusion, give them a big bonus in the form of another cookie.)

Step 2

Play a "secular" song in which someone promises to "be there" for someone else. Possibilities include "I'll Be There" (Mariah Carey), "I'll Be Your Everything" (Tommy Page), "Bridge Over Troubled Water" (Simon and Garfunkel), "That's What Friends Are For" (Dionne Warwick and Friends), "I'll Be Loving You (Forever)" (New Kids on the Block), "Forever Your Girl" (Paula Abdul), and "Before the Next Teardrop Falls" (Freddy Fender). Ask: **What is the singer promising to do? How might the world be different if every person had that kind of commitment from someone else? On a scale of one to ten—with ten being the highest—how much support do you think most kids in our group get from each other? How could we improve that?**

Step 5

Before the session, purchase two "recordable" greeting cards—the kind containing a small recording device that captures any spoken greeting you care to put on it. The greeting plays when the card is opened. To close the meeting, have kids form two teams. Put the teams in separate rooms. Give each team a card. Instruct each team to record an encouraging message for the other team—one that pledges support during the coming week. The message may be spoken or sung. Then regather the group and have teams trade cards. Allow kids to pass the cards around so that they can listen to the messages individually.

Step 1

Replace Steps 1 and 2 with a shorter opener. Have kids form pairs. Instruct the pairs to line up against one wall. Partners must face each other and hold hands. Give each pair a helium-filled balloon with no string. The challenge for each pair is to get its balloon from one side of the room to the other, holding the balloon between the partners' noses. Award a prize to any successful team. Afterward, ask: **What was the secret of winning this game?** (Working together; paying attention to what your partner was doing; going slowly.) **Does anybody put that kind of effort into helping you get from one end of the week to the other? If so, who? What if the members of this group put that kind of effort into helping you? How might your week be different?** Instead of using Repro Resource 7, ask kids where and when during the week it would be best to have another Christian close by—and why.

Step 3

Skip the II Corinthians 6:14-18 reading and discussion. Instead, read Romans 12:10, 13, 15, 16 and relate it to the human pyramid activity. Skip Steps 4 and 5. Instead, put one group member in the middle of the room and have the rest of the group pose supportively around him or her—arms on shoulders, smiling at the person, etc. Take a Polaroid photo of this and give it to the person in the center. Do the same for each group member, giving each a turn in the center. Have kids take their photos home as reminders of the support available in your group. If time allows, choose accountability partners (Step 4) and share the Post-it™ note idea.

Step 4

Ask volunteers from your church—people of widely varying ages—to come to your meeting to share with your group members why fellowship with other Christians is so important to them. Help your kids see that Christian fellowship is for people of all ages. Before you dismiss your volunteers, give your group members an opportunity to ask them some questions.

Step 5

If many of your group members come from broken homes, close the session by affirming that Christians are part of the *family* of God. Read Mark 3:31-35. Point out that the bonds and relationships that can—and should—be formed by Christians are every bit as strong as natural family bonds. As a group, sing a couple of hymns or songs that address the topic of the Christian family. (Amy Grant's song "Family" is a good example.)

Step 1
Instead of playing "The Swarm," have kids share some examples of times when they felt out of place or "under attack." Especially encourage your high schoolers to share situations they faced when in junior high. List the situations on the board as group members mention them. Then talk about why kids felt the way they did, asking others in the group to share about similar experiences. Finally, discuss what your kids might be able to do to avoid such situations in the future.

Step 2
Instead of using Repro Resource 7, bring in a large, wall-sized piece of paper on which you've written "Of the Minority in Majority U.S.A." Instruct kids to draw scenes depicting areas of their lives in which they feel they are in the minority. This could include anything from not caring about what brand of shoes you wear in a name-brand-shoe culture to not wanting to be part of a "gossip chain." When the wall is complete, talk about how it feels to be in the minority in such a majority-driven culture. Then ask: **What do you think we can do about this?**

Step 4
The ironic, exaggerated humor of Repro Resource 8 may be lost on your sixth graders. So instead of using the sheet, simply ask: **What are some things non-Christians do for fun that Christians aren't allowed to do? Do you think it's fair that non-Christians can do things that Christians aren't allowed to do? Why or why not? Do you think non-Christians have more fun than Christians do? Be honest.** Get several responses; then move on to the brainstorming activity at the end of Step 4.

Step 5
Before the session, you'll need to prepare for each of your group members a list of the unique or special qualities he or she brings to your group's fellowship. As you close the session, share your lists with your kids in front of the whole group. Let your kids know that each of them brings something special to your fellowship. So when he or she is gone, something is missing from your group.

Date Used:

Approx. Time

Step 1: Staying Alive Outside the Hive _____
o Small Group
o Heard It All Before
o Fellowship & Worship
o Mostly Girls
o Short Meeting Time
o Combined Junior High/High School
Things needed:

Step 2: Swimming Upstream in a Downstream World _____
o Extra Action
o Little Bible Background
o Mostly Guys
o Extra Fun
o Media
o Combined Junior High/High School
Things needed:

Step 3: Swords, Pyramids, and Lawnmower Blades _____
o Large Group
o Heard It All Before
o Little Bible Background
o Short Meeting Time
Things needed:

Step 4: The Fun Factor _____
o Extra Action
o Small Group
o Large Group
o Mostly Girls
o Urban
o Sixth Grade
Things needed:

Step 5: Strength in Numbers _____
o Fellowship & Worship
o Mostly Guys
o Extra Fun
o Media
o Urban
o Sixth Grade
Things needed:

5 Why Serve Others?

YOUR GOALS FOR THIS SESSION:

Choose one or more

☐ To help kids recognize that serving God often involves serving others.

☐ To help kids understand that faith without actions is dead.

☐ To help motivate and prepare kids to plan and carry out acts of Christian service.

☐ Other _____
_____

Your Bible Base:

Matthew 25:31-46
Luke 10:25-37
Ephesians 6:7, 8
James 2:14-26

Bake That Cake!

(Needed: Cake ingredients, utensils, timer)

If possible, begin your meeting in a kitchen area. If it's not possible to meet in a kitchen area, you'll need to bring cake-baking ingredients and utensils, as well as a cake that you've baked before the session. (But don't bring out the cake until the end of the session.)

Ask: **How many of you like to eat cake? How many of you like making cakes?** After kids respond, explain that there is going to be a cake-baking contest, pitting the guys against the girls (if possible). You'll need two sets of ingredients and utensils for baking a cake.

Explain: **When I say, "Go," both teams will have five minutes to get their cake prepared. Ready! Set! Go!**

This five-minute period could be a bit chaotic, particularly if some of the team members have never baked before. Ideally, both teams will start by reading the recipe on the cake mix box and following the instructions. Occasionally, you may want to call out how much time is left. After five minutes, declare a winner based on how how close each team came to completing the recipe. (If you're in a kitchen area, be sure you know how much time it will take the cakes to bake, so you can return to the kitchen to take them out of the oven.)

Afterward, ask: **If both teams had just stood around and not done anything, would the cakes have gotten made?** (Of course not.)

Explain: **Even though both teams had everything that was needed to make a cake, they had to *do* something to actually make the cake happen.**

STEP 2

In Word and Deed

(Needed: Bibles, copies of Repro Resource 9, pencils,)

Ask one of your girls to stand at the front of the room. Say: **Let's say that _____ plans to start working out at the local fitness center. She buys some cross-training shoes, exercise outfits, and a Walkman headset so that she "looks the part." She even reads up on exercises, so she'll know how to do them. Yet with all this preparation, she never actually exercises.**

Ask one of your guys to stand at the front of the room. Say: **Let's say that _____ plans to run for president of the United States. He studies the issues, hits the campaign trail to win voters, and after several long years, is finally elected president. On Inauguration Day, he gets sworn in, making him official. But he does nothing—not one solitary act—as president!**

Point out that in both cases, the people didn't act on what they had prepared themselves to do.

Ask your kids how these examples might relate to Christians who don't serve and act on their faith. If no one mentions it, point out that some people become Christians and start growing and being discipled in the faith, learning more and more about how God wants us to live. Yet with all of God's resources at their fingertips, they don't act on them.

Have kids turn in their Bibles to James 2:14-26. Ask for a volunteer to read the passage aloud. Afterward, say: **James has some strong words to Christians who aren't acting on their faith!**

Ask your kids to reflect on their current spiritual state, answering silently the following questions: **Based on what we've just read, how alive would you say your faith is right now, on a scale of one to ten? What have you done or what are you doing for the kingdom of God?**

Ask your kids what comes to mind when they think of doing "deeds" for the kingdom of God. As kids respond, see if the idea of being a missionary overseas comes up. Ask your kids why some people think that serving God necessarily means going overseas on the mission field. After kids respond, explain that you're going to look at some other options of Christian service besides the mission field.

Have kids turn to Matthew 25:31-46. Ask someone to read the

passage aloud. Afterward, ask for enough volunteers to fill the parts in the skit "Sheep or Goat?" (Repro Resource 9). Assign the parts and hand out copies of the sheet to the performers. Give volunteers a few minutes to read through the skit before performing it.

When the skit is finished, ask your kids what they would do if God Himself asked them for something to eat, drink, or wear or asked them to visit Him.

After kids respond, ask: **Why do you think some Christians ignore the basic needs of people in society, even though God says that if we do things for these people, in essence, we're doing them for Him?**

After kids comment, say: **It seems that the point God is trying to get across to us is that to serve Him, we must serve others. Let's find out who these "others" are that God is specifically referring to.**

Just Who Exactly Is My Neighbor?

(Needed: Bibles, copies of Repro Resource 10, pencils)

Ask your kids to close their eyes and picture the neighborhood where they live. Ask them if they can name all of their neighbors—not the ones five or six houses down the street, but the ones who live next to them or across the street from them. Go around the room, asking your kids to try to name their neighbors.

Afterward, assign one of your kids to read the story of the Good Samaritan in Luke 10:25-37. But first, have the person read just verse 27. Say: **This man knew Jesus' command to "love your neighbor as yourself." But a couple of verses later, the man asks Jesus, "Who is my neighbor?" Who do you think Jesus was referring to when He said to love your neighbor?** Let kids respond.

Before you have your group member read the rest of the passage, assign some of your kids to play the characters in the Good Samaritan story. These characters might include the man who was beaten and robbed, the robbers, the priest, the Levite, the Samaritan, and the innkeeper. (You might even let someone be the donkey if you want.) Have kids act out the passage as the person reads it.

Afterward, discuss with your kids whether or not they think the story defines exactly who our neighbors are. Ask for their conclusions on

what this parable is saying. Then point out that instead of nailing down who is and isn't our neighbor, this story indicates that we are to show merciful acts of service to everyone we come in contact with.

Suggest that instead of figuring out which people we have to serve and which people we don't, Christian service is more of an *attitude*. This attitude can be best summed up as being concerned with and acting on other people's interests, and not just our own (Philippians 2:4).

Ask: **In what areas might it be difficult for you to think of other people's needs rather than your own?** Get several responses.

Ask your kids to name some needs that other students at their school might have that they could possibly help meet. Then hand out copies of "Coming Soon to a School Near You" (Repro Resource 10). Allow a few minutes for kids to create a modern-day Good Samaritan example that could happen at their school. After a few minutes, allow each kid to read his or her modern-day parable to the group.

STEP

4

Get Those Hands Dirty!

(Needed: Bibles, previously baked cake [optional])

Refer back to the Good Samaritan passage in Luke 10:25-37. This time, ask your reader to read only the last four words of verse 37 ("Go and do likewise"). Then say: **Jesus didn't say to the man, "Think about this"; He said, "Go and do likewise."**

Explain to your kids the benefits that come from service to others. Have someone read aloud Matthew 25:34 for a glimpse of the inheritance that God promises for us.

Afterward, say: **That inheritance may sound inviting, but what benefits does Christian service have for people *right now*?** Have someone read aloud Ephesians 6:7, 8, which promises that "the Lord will reward everyone for whatever good he does."

Let kids discuss their feelings regarding the promises and benefits God gives us both now and in the future. Then ask: **Even with all of these benefits from God for those who serve others in Christ, why do you think some people are reluctant to serve?** (Some people are selfish, and only want to satisfy themselves. Some people believe they are too busy to serve others. Some people may be afraid of being thought of as weird for serving others.)

OPTIONS

EXTRA ACTION

SMALL GROUP

LARGE GROUP

HEARD IT ALL BEFORE

LITTLE BIBLE BACKGROUND

FELLOWSHIP & WORSHIP

EXTRA FUN

MEDIA

JR.HIGH HIGH SCHOOL COMBINED

After some discussion, brainstorm as a group some ways that your group members can serve others. You may want to refer back to Matthew 25:31-46 for a whole list of ideas. Your kids could help out at a homeless shelter or at a soup kitchen by serving meals. They could collect food and clothing to take to a local shelter. You could plan to visit a local nursing home, where your kids could talk with the patients and sing songs to them. You could plan a weekend activity in which your kids could help with a local work team. Rebuilding a fence or a garage, doing yard work, and painting are all options that would no doubt be welcomed by members of your community.

Regardless of the activities your group plans, emphasize that serving God is a constant attitude. And whether it's at home, at school, or with friends, we must be primed and ready to take on the interests of those in need.

Close the session by making your way back to the church kitchen to eat the cakes that have been baking (or simply serve the cake that you baked before the session).

SHEEP or GOAT?

Setting: Billy and Jane are unwinding from a long day. Billy's sitting in a chair, reading the paper. Jane is on the couch, thumbing through a book.

JANE *(answering the phone)*: Hello. Yes, this is the Goats residence. *(Sits up excitedly)* This is who? You mean, as in Jesus, the Son of God? *(Billy drops the paper, quickly jumping over to the couch where Jane is sitting.)* You say You're coming over? Tonight? Uh, OK, we'll look forward to seeing You. *(Hangs up phone.)*

BILLY: Jesus is coming over? Tonight? To our house?

JANE: That's what He said. Can you believe it? Jesus! *(Both stare around the room and then look back at each other.)*

BILLY & JANE: We've got to clean this place up! *(Both begin frantically straightening furniture, dusting, and vacuuming.)*

JANE: He'll have to eat something. You go get some food ready. I just went grocery shopping, so the refrigerator is full.

BILLY: OK. Can you get out one of my new sweaters? We have to look nice for Jesus. You should wear one of those new outfits you just bought. They're just sitting in the closet. *(Jane nods her head. Then both go back to buzzing around the house, cleaning and preparing. The doorbell rings.)*

BILLY & JANE: He's here! *(Billy tries his best to straighten his clothing, takes a breath, and opens the front door.)*

HUNGRY MAN *(begging in a pathetic voice as he stands in the doorway)*: Good sir, could you spare something to eat and drink? I haven't had a thing in days. Just some bread and water, please.

BILLY *(cutting the man off impatiently)*: I don't have anything to give you. Besides, we're expecting a guest any minute now. So please leave. *(Billy closes the door before the man can respond.)* I'm getting tired of people coming around here begging. Why don't people like that just get a job? *(Jane hands Billy his sweater, which he puts on. Both sit down, waiting for their guest to arrive. The doorbell rings again. Billy runs across the room, then slowly opens the door.)*

COLD MAN *(collapsing on his knees in the doorway, shivering)*: Sir, do you have any clothes to spare? I think I've got frostbite.

BILLY *(quickly pushing the man out the door)*: I'm sorry, we just donated all of our extra clothes to the Salvation Army last week. There's a local shelter just down the street. Why don't you try there? *(Billy blows into his hands, trying to warm up.)* Wow, it's freezing out there!

JANE: It sure is. That guy must be insane to be out with no coat on. Who taught him how to dress? *(Jane and Billy go back to their reading, but frequently check their watches.)* I wonder what's keeping Jesus. *(Doorbell rings again.)*

BILLY & JANE: That's got to be Him. *(Both walk to the door with warm smiles on their faces and open the door.)*

LONELY MAN *(in a sad voice)*: I'm sorry to bother you, kind folks, but I just need somebody to talk to. Today marks one year since my wife left me. Could I come in and—

JANE: You know, there are professionals you should probably talk to. We're not qualified to help you out. We'll pray for you, though. Have a good night. *(Closes the door.)*

BILLY: That's too bad. But I'm glad we're still together. I wonder what's keeping Jesus. It's kind of rude—He hasn't bothered to call or anything to say that He'd be late. *(The phone rings. Billy answers it.)* Hello? Hi, Jesus. Where have you been? . . . That's impossible, we've been here all night.

VOICE OF JESUS: Depart from me, you who are cursed. . . . For I was hungry and you gave me nothing to eat, I was thirsty and you gave me nothing to drink, I was a stranger and you did not invite me in, I needed clothes and you did not clothe me. . . . They also will answer, "Lord, when did we see you hungry or thirsty or a stranger or needing clothes . . . and did not help you?" He will reply, "I tell you the truth, whatever you did not do for one of the least of these, you did not do for me."

(Billy and Jane both have their ears to the phone, but are standing frozen, looking shocked and scared. A loud click is heard on the other end of the line.)

Coming Soon to a School Near You

OK, so maybe a gang of thieves wouldn't rob and beat up somebody at your school and leave the person lying in the hallway. But there are probably situations that occur every day at your school that are *similar* to the Good Samaritan story.

Create a short story—set in your school—that reflects the basic principle of the Good Samaritan story. Your scenario may be serious or humorous. Take a few minutes to write your story in the space below. Be prepared to share it with the group.

Step 2

Before reading the James passage, try a demonstration of faith and works. Put a water-filled tub or large bucket in the middle of your meeting area. Have a towel handy. Say: **I can walk on water. I can also enable any person in this room to walk on water! I'll give a prize to any person who lets me enable him or her to walk on water right now. You have to leave your shoes and socks on, but I promise they won't get soaked.** See what happens. (You might want to let a couple of group members in on this stunt beforehand if you think no one else will volunteer.) Have volunteers stand in line by the water. Then bring out a tray of ice cubes that you've been hiding. Put the towel on the floor, dump the ice on the towel, and you and your volunteers can walk across the frozen water. After awarding prizes, discuss the difference between believing that it's possible to walk on water and actually doing it.

Step 4

Instead of discussing a theoretical service project, tackle one right in your meeting place. Depending on where you are and what needs doing, you could have group members clean the place up, fold church bulletins, make cards for shut-ins, change diapers in the church nursery, or give a bath to a youth sponsor's dog. If time allows, talk afterward about who was served by the project you undertook.

Step 3

In the context of the good Samaritan story, encourage group members to think of each other as "neighbors." Too often small groups remain small because there's plenty of room for members to "keep their distance" from each other. Unity must begin in your group before it will spread effectively to others at school. If you don't believe your own group is as close as it should be, have everyone share a specific need with the rest of the group. Write all of the needs on the board. Then see if anyone is willing to agree to pray for or attend to those needs in other ways. All those who are willing should sign an agreement.

Step 4

When you're planning service activities, don't forget the individual homes of your group members. Many times the church looks to traditional outlets of service such as those listed in the session. But some of your kids may come from homes that could use help with cleaning, baby-sitting, grocery shopping, or other kinds of chores that your group members could do on a weekend. If your own group members have unmet needs, it's going to be difficult for them to begin meeting the needs of other people.

Step 3

Before the session, you'll need to cut apart four maps of the United States (or another country). Put the pieces of each map into an envelope (so that you have four envelopes). At the beginning of Step 3, have kids form four teams. Give each team one of the envelopes. Have the teams compete to see which one can correctly reassemble its map first. You may be surprised at how little your kids know about areas outside of their region! Afterward, ask: **Do you feel like you have any responsibility to the people in other regions of the country? If so, what is your responsibility? If not, why not?** Compare group members' answers with Jesus' response to the young man who asked Him, "Who is my neighbor?"

Step 4

If you have time at the end of the session, consider involving your kids in an impromptu service project. Take your group to an area near your meeting place that's full of litter. Have kids form teams. Give each team three bags: one to collect cans, one to collect paper, and one to collect other garbage. Set a time limit and let teams collect as much litter as possible. When time is up, see which team collected the most litter. Award prizes, if you wish.

HEARD IT ALL BEFORE

Step 3

If you've studied the Good Samaritan recently, skip that passage. Instead, have kids brainstorm a list of "The Five Nicest People in the Bible." (The list might include Jesus, Dorcas, Barnabas, Jonathan, Mary the mother of Jesus, etc.) Discuss how these people served others. (Let kids use a concordance or Bible dictionary to find information about the characters, if needed.) Then brainstorm a list of "The Five Nastiest People in the Bible" (The list might include Satan, Judas, Herod, Pharaoh, Cain, etc.) Discuss the selfishness of these characters. Use your findings to illustrate the fact that servanthood, unlike selfishness, is a quality most people admire.

Step 4

After hearing at school and in the media about the needs of the hungry, the homeless, victims of war, and others, kids may feel overwhelmed and ready to tune out. Rather than listing all of the world's needs and trying to pick one to address, choose one need yourself before the session. Give the need a human face by bringing in an acquaintance who has firsthand experience with meeting the need—a missionary who has seen famine, a volunteer from a crisis pregnancy center, or someone who has a relative in prison, for example. Ask your acquaintance to talk briefly to the group and to suggest specific ways in which your group could help. Choose one of those ways and concentrate on how you'll carry out your plan during the next few weeks.

LITTLE BIBLE BACKGROUND

Step 2

The account of the sheep and goats in Matthew 25:31-46 can be a bit scary if this is the first time your group members are dealing with it. Don't rush through it. You'll probably want to do more in response than simply read through Repro Resource 9. Begin by encouraging kids to ask questions of their own. If you don't get much response, then *you* need to ask enough questions to make sure that kids have a clear understanding of what Jesus is saying. Explain that Jesus tells this story not to judge us for the mistakes of our past, but to help us make better decisions in the future. While most people can probably recall past instances in which they could have helped someone but didn't, the important thing to remember is that they begin *now* to see the needs of other people more as Jesus sees them.

Step 4

For people with little Bible background, the Book of James is an excellent read-through book. First, however, you may need to offer help with the references in Step 2 (James 2:14-26) to Abraham, Isaac, and Rahab. Deal with questions about today's assignment; then ask your group members to read the Book of James in its entirety this week and give you a report on it—in twenty-five words or less—at your next meeting. Most of what James has to say is straightforward and clear. *What* he says is likely to raise some questions, but how he says it makes his book a good one for groups like yours to examine on their own.

FELLOWSHIP & WORSHIP

Step 1

Before kids arrive, set out bowls of warm water, each with a washcloth and towel, at various places throughout your meeting area. If possible, have enough bowls to be able to pair up your kids and assign each pair a bowl. When kids arrive, set them up with their bowls and have them wash each others' feet. When they're done splashing around, ask what typically comes to mind when they hear someone mention Christian service. If no one mentions it, bring up foot-washing. Say: **Jesus' act of washing His disciples' feet was an example He gave us for serving, but that doesn't mean that's the way *we* are to serve.** Talk about the many different ways that we can serve Christ through everyday activities. Then ask: **Why do you think God wants us to serve others?** Get several responses. Then move on to Step 2 in the session.

Step 4

Hand out paper and pencils. Instruct each person to write a psalm of service. If kids wish, they may use Psalm 150 (a psalm of praise) as an example. When everyone is finished, ask volunteers to share their psalms with the rest of the group. Close the session in prayer, thanking God for the opportunities He gives us to serve Him.

MOSTLY GIRLS

Step 1

If you don't have enough guys in your group for a girls-versus-guys contest, split your girls into two teams and pit them against each other. You may want to make the contest a bit more of a challenge by having group members bake cakes from scratch, rather than from a mix. Be sure that your girls know that you'll be taste-testing these cakes at the end of the session!

Step 2

For a group of mostly girls, you'll probably want to make some changes to the skit on Repro Resource 9. Change the character of "Billy" to "Janet." Change the setting of the skit from a living room to a college dorm room. Explain that Janet and Jane are twins who have always done everything together—including rooming together at college. The visitors (the hungry person, the cold person, and the lonely person) may all be other female college students. For the voice of Jesus, you may wish to recruit a male from your church to speak that part. The rest of the skit should work well as written.

MOSTLY GUYS

Step 1

Before you assemble in the kitchen, give your guys an unopened Frisbee and ask them to throw it around outside. After they rip open the package and give the Frisbee a couple of tosses, send them to the kitchen for the cake-baking competition. Afterward, ask: **Why didn't you read the instructions before throwing the Frisbee? Why *did* you read the instructions on the box before making the cake?** Point out the importance of reading instructions to learn how to do new things. Unless your group members are convinced they know all there is to know about living a good Christian life, challenge them to keep reading until it becomes as natural to them as throwing a Frisbee.

Step 2

After you discuss the importance of taking action in the Christian life, have your guys create a slogan that they can use to motivate themselves (and each other) in the future. If time permits, have them make a banner with their new slogan on it to post in your meeting area for a while. Depending on your guys' creative abilities, you might even have them write a song that incorporates the slogan, design sweatshirts that feature it, or do something else to help them remember it on a daily (rather than a weekly) basis.

EXTRA FUN

Step 1

Begin the session by announcing that you want to play a couple of board games. One should be a game that's familiar to everyone—something that group members open up and start playing right away. The other should be a new or unusual game that no one has ever heard of—but one you're sure that your group members will like. Arrange to leave the room at about the time kids start the second game. See if anyone is willing to read through all of the instructions to learn how to play. Afterward, compare the games to Christian living. Point out that both games can be equally fun, but until we get familiar with another set of rules, one might seem a lot harder than the other. Similarly, we do certain things as Christians that we get used to and that begin to come naturally. But if we carefully read the "instructions" on how to live—the Bible—we may discover new opportunities that are just as good or even better than what we already know.

Step 4

Change your opening activity from a cake-baking contest to a cookie-baking contest. If you bake a large batch of cookies, all of your group members can have samples—and then they can also have a lot of fun sharing the cookies with other people. Come up with a quick list of possible recipients (your pastor, other church members, your church janitor, etc.), pile into a few cars, and make some on-the-spot deliveries. You've just been discussing how people should take action in their Christian lives. If you now prove that doing so can be a lot of fun, your group members are a lot more likely to "go and do likewise."

Step 3

To illustrate that the "Who is my neighbor?" question has gotten more complicated since New Testament days, try one of the following activities. (1) Before the session, find a group member or an adult from your church who subscribes to an on-line computer service (such as CompuServe, Prodigy, America Online, eWorld, etc.). Ask the person to demonstrate how the service puts the user in touch with faraway people who can become electronic "neighbors."
(2) Arrange to have an acquaintance fax a family photo (with names, ages, etc.) to your meeting place. Pass around the faxed photo for your group members to look at. After using one of these choices, ask: **Who is your neighbor now? Should we try not to find out about people and needs around the world so that we don't have to do anything about them? What do you think Jesus would do?**

Step 4

Play one or more contemporary Christian songs that issue a call to serve others. Possibilities include "Hollow Eyes" (Petra), "Doer of the Word" (Dan Peek), "Somebody's Brother" (Scott Wesley Brown), "Mountain Top" (Amy Grant), and "Vital Signs" (White Heart). After the song(s), ask: **How did this music make you feel? Let's say the singer or singers come to our meeting two weeks from now and say, "What did you do in response to that song?" What would you like to be able to answer?**

Step 1

Skip the cake-baking. Before the session, make (or have a few kids make) several signs prohibiting virtually every activity that might take place during a typical meeting ("No Running," "No Eating," "No Sitting," "No Laughing," "No Volleyball," "No Making Fun of the Leader," "No Reading Signs," etc.). Post the signs in your meeting place. As kids enter, appoint a few to help you enforce the rules; anyone caught breaking a rule is sent to "jail" (the corner). If anyone is still at liberty when you're ready to start the meeting, give that person a prize "for being the best at doing nothing." Ask: **Is this what being a Christian is all about—doing nothing?** After listening to replies, move directly to the James passage in Step 2.

Step 3

Skip Step 3. At the start of Step 4, summarize (or have a volunteer summarize) the Good Samaritan story before reading the last four words of Luke 10:37. Instead of planning a group service project, hand out index cards and pens. Say: **Think of someone at school or in our group whom you've tended to ignore—almost as if you were walking past that person on the road. On your card, write three needs that person might have. Then circle the need that might be easiest for you to meet.** Give kids a minute to pray silently about how they could help meet that need this week.

Step 1

If you don't have access to a kitchen for the baking activity, try another opener. Ask kids to think about the hardest job they've ever completed—the hardest work they've ever done in their lives. One at a time, have kids come to the front of the room to act out (charades-style) his or her tough job for the rest of the group to guess. After all of the jobs have been guessed, ask: **If you'd just stood around and not done anything, would your job have gotten done?** (Of course not.) Explain: **You had to _do_ something to actually complete your job.** Then move on to Step 2.

Step 3

Before you get into the story of the Good Samaritan in Step 3, pass around several articles (which you've clipped from newspapers and newsmagazines) that deal with international events, preferably ones that involve a need. Give kids a chance to read a few of the articles. Then say: **Jesus tells us to love our neighbors as ourselves. After reading these articles, who would you say our "neighbors" are? Why?** Get several opinions; then take a look at how Jesus responded to the question.

Step 2
Before you read the Scripture references, ask: **What are some problems you see in the world that you would like to have changed? It could any problem from world hunger to the kid sitting next to you in algebra class who always cheats.** List group members' problems on the board as they're named. Then refer back to Step 2 in the session and work through the Scripture passages and questions listed there. When you're finished, come back to your master list. Ask: **From what we've just read and learned, what do you think we could do about these problems?** Encourage kids to come up with practical, realistic solutions. If there's one thing they're particularly excited about, you may even want to adopt it as a group project.

Step 4
As you're brainstorming ideas that your group members could take on as a service project, set up a challenge. Divide your group into two teams—a team of junior highers and a team of high schoolers. Challenge the members of each team to decide on one service project that they could do in the next month. At the end of the month, be sure to get a report of what they decided on and how it went.

Step 1
If you'd rather not have your sixth graders playing around with cake ingredients, try another opening activity. Have kids form two or three groups. Give each group a snap-together model kit. Have the groups compete to see which one can put its model together first. Award prizes to the first group that finishes. Afterward, ask: **If the members of your group had just stood around and not done anything, would the models have been completed?** (Of course not.) Explain: **Even though your group had everything that was needed to build a model, you had to *do* something to actually get the model built.** Then move on to Step 2.

Step 3
Explore the concept of "neighbors" in a little more detail with your sixth graders. Ask: **Who are your neighbors at home?** See how many kids can name the people who live around them. **Who are your neighbors at school?** See how many kids can name the people they sit next to in class or the kids whose lockers are next to theirs. **Who are our neighbors here at church?** See how many kids can name the people or establishments around your church. **Who are our state neighbors?** See how many kids can name the states that surround yours. **Who are our national neighbors?** See how many kids can name the countries that border yours. Use these questions to lead in to a discussion of Jesus' response to the young man who asked Him, "Who is my neighbor?"

Date Used:

Approx.
Time
_____

Step 1: Bake That Cake!
o Fellowship & Worship
o Mostly Girls
o Mostly Guys
o Extra Fun
o Short Meeting Time
o Urban
o Sixth Grade
Things needed:

Step 2: In Word and Deed _____
o Extra Action
o Little Bible Background
o Mostly Girls
o Mostly Guys
o Combined Junior High/High School
Things needed:

Step 3: Just Who Exactly Is My Neighbor? _____
o Small Group
o Large Group
o Heard It All Before
o Media
o Short Meeting Time
o Urban
o Sixth Grade
Things needed:

Step 4: Get Those Hands Dirty! _____
o Extra Action
o Small Group
o Large Group
o Heard It All Before
o Little Bible Background
o Fellowship & Worship
o Extra Fun
o Media
o Combined Junior High/High School
Things needed:

Custom Curriculum Critique

Please take a moment to fill out this evaluation form, rip it out, fold it, tape it, and send it back to us. This will help us continue to customize products for you. Thanks!

1. Overall, please give this *Custom Curriculum* course (*Extreme Closeup*) a grade in terms of how well it worked for you. (A=excellent; B=above average; C=average; D=below average; F=failure) Circle one.

    A B C D F

2. Now assign a grade to each part of this curriculum that you used.

a. Upfront article	A B C D F	Didn't use
b. Publicity/Clip art	A B C D F	Didn't use
c. Repro Resource Sheets	A B C D F	Didn't use
d. Session 1	A B C D F	Didn't use
e. Session 2	A B C D F	Didn't use
f. Session 3	A B C D F	Didn't use
g. Session 4	A B C D F	Didn't use
h. Session 5	A B C D F	Didn't use

3. How helpful were the options?
    - ❏ Very helpful
    - ❏ Somewhat helpful
    - ❏ Not too helpful
    - ❏ Not at all helpful

4. Rate the amount of options:
    - ❏ Too many
    - ❏ About the right amount
    - ❏ Too few

5. Tell us how often you used each type of option (4=Always; 3=Sometimes; 2=Seldom; 1=Never)

	4	3	2	1
Extra Action	❏	❏	❏	❏
Combined Jr. High/High School	❏	❏	❏	❏
Urban	❏	❏	❏	❏
Small Group	❏	❏	❏	❏
Large Group	❏	❏	❏	❏
Extra Fun	❏	❏	❏	❏
Heard It All Before	❏	❏	❏	❏
Little Bible Background	❏	❏	❏	❏
Short Meeting Time	❏	❏	❏	❏
Fellowship and Worship	❏	❏	❏	❏
Mostly Guys	❏	❏	❏	❏
Mostly Girls	❏	❏	❏	❏
Media	❏	❏	❏	❏
Extra Challenge (High School only)	❏	❏	❏	❏
Sixth Grade (Jr. High only)	❏	❏	❏	❏

6. What did you like best about this course?

7. What suggestions do you have for improving *Custom Curriculum*?

8. Other topics you'd like to see covered in this series:

9. Are you?
   ❏ Full time paid youthworker
   ❏ Part time paid youthworker
   ❏ Volunteer youthworker

10. When did you use *Custom Curriculum*?
    ❏ Sunday School   ❏ Small Group
    ❏ Youth Group   ❏ Retreat
    ❏ Other _____

11. What grades did you use it with? _____

12. How many kids used the curriculum in an average week? _____

13. What's the approximate attendance of your entire Sunday school program (Nursery through Adult)? _____

14. If you would like information on other *Custom Curriculum* courses, or other youth products from David C. Cook, please fill out the following:

Name: _____

Church Name: _____

Address: _____
_____

Phone: (____) _____

Thank you!